BRONX PRIMITIVE

For Anne
with Love from Is
N.Y.C.
8/8/85

BRONX PRIMITIVE

Portraits in a Childhood

Kate Simon

HARPER COLOPHON BOOKS

HARPER & ROW, PUBLISHERS

NEW YORK, CAMBRIDGE, PHILADELPHIA, SAN FRANCISCO

LONDON, MEXICO CITY, SAO PAULO, SYDNEY

Grateful acknowledgment is made to the following for permission to reprint copyrighted material:

Irving Berlin Music Corporation: Excerpt from "Because I Love You" by Irving Berlin, p. 88; copyright 1926 by Irving Berlin, renewed. Excerpt from "Always" by Irving Berlin, p. 88; copyright 1925 by Irving Berlin, renewed. Excerpt from "Remember" by Irving Berlin, p. 109; copyright 1925 by Irving Berlin, renewed. Used by permission, all rights reserved.

A hardcover edition of this book is published by The Viking Press. It is here reprinted by arrangement.

First HARPER COLOPHON edition published 1983.

Library of Congress Cataloging in Publication Data

Simon, Kate.
    Bronx primitive.

    (Harper colophon books)
    1. Simon, Kate.   2. Jews—New York (N.Y.)—Biography.
3. Bronx (New York, N.Y.)—Biography.   4. New York (N.Y.)
—Biography.   I. Title.
F128.9.J5S57   1983   974.7'27504'0924 [B]   83-47572
ISBN: 0-06-091067-4 (pbk.)   (previously ISBN: 0-670-19239-2)

84 85 86 10 9 8 7 6 5 4 3

For Alex and Mark Kajitani

Contents

BRONX
PRIMITIVE

1

Lafontaine Near Tremont

We lived at 2029 Lafontaine, the last house on the west side of the street from 178th to 179th, a row of five-story tenements that ended at a hat factory. To the north and solidly, interminably, along the block to 180th there stretched a bitter ugliness of high walls of big stones that held a terminal point and service barns of El trains. (It may be that my recoil from early Renaissance palaces, their pugnacious blocks of stone and fortress grimness, stems from these inimical El walls.) Across from the factory were a garage and the Italian frame houses that lined that side of the street down to 178th Street. At the corner of 178th Street, on our Jewish-German-Polish-Greek-Hungarian-Rumanian side, was Mrs. Katz's candy store. The only other store I knew at first was the grocery run by a plodding elderly couple at the corner of 179th Street and Arthur Avenue, the street to the east. In spite of their lack of English and my frail Yiddish, I eagerly ran errands there to watch their feet slide and pat in their brown felt slippers and to admire the precision with which the old man cut once, twice, into a tub of butter to dig out exactly a quarter pound.

And on their side of 179th Street, about midway between Arthur and Lafontaine, there was a big tree, the only street tree in the neighborhood, which showered me, and only me, with a million white blossoms. It was my tree and I watched and touched it as carefully as the Italian grandfathers watched and touched the tomato plants in their backyards.

Our station of the El was Tremont, which was numerically 177th Street, and Main Street. Between dark Third Avenue and its changing grids and slashes of light and Lafontaine, there was Monterey Avenue, on its west side a row of tenements and on its east, running from 178th to 179th, a resplendent, high empty lot, as full of possibilities as a park. It had patches of daisies and buttercups, plumy and scratchy bushes; on its eastern edge and below our fire escapes, seductive glittering objects thrown from Lafontaine windows—a shining knife handle, red glass and blue glass, bits of etched cut glass. Once my brother and I found a seltzer bottle nozzle and once a Chinese record, a wonderment we played over and over again on the Victrola, until our parents, impatient with the repetition of high thin notes with startling starts and stops, caused it to disappear. There were two ways of getting onto the lot: 178th Street was an easy, gradual slope; 179th Street was jutting rock for a height of two stories. The few girls who managed it were never quite the same again, a little more defiant, a little more impudent.

To the west of Lafontaine was Arthur Avenue, a mixture of Jewish tenements and frame houses in which lived Italian families and a number of Irish. Beyond was Belmont, whose only significance was that it held, at its meeting with Tremont, the movie house we all trooped to on Saturday after lunch. The other movie house, which offered a combination of films and vaudeville, was a rare pleasure; it cost more and was saved for special occasions, a birthday or a report card that said A for work, A for effort, A for conduct.

This theater for celebrations was also on Tremont, toward the west, not far from Webster Avenue, beyond Bathgate and Washington. Bathgate, moving southward from Tremont toward Claremont Parkway, was the market street where mothers bought yard goods early in the week, as well as dried mushrooms and shoelaces. On Wednesdays they bought chickens and live fish to swim in the bathtub until Friday, when they became gefilte fish. Most women plucked their own chickens. A few aristocrats, like my mother and Mrs. Horowitz (who spoke English perfectly, the only Jewish woman we knew who did), paid a little dark bundle in a dusty red wig ten cents to pluck fast, her hand like the needle of a sewing machine, up down, up down, as a red and black and white garden of feathers spread at her feet. On the next block, Washington, was the public library, and a block north of it, on the corner with Tremont, the barber shop where I went for my Buster Brown haircut. Tremont west of Third also held the delectable five-and-ten, crisscrosses of rainbows and pots of gold.

Our suburbs, our summer country homes, our camps, our banks and braes, our America the Beautiful, our fields of gaming and dalliance and voyeurism, were in Crotona Park, whose northern border fronted on Tremont Avenue.

Our apartment, 5B, was a top-floor railroad flat, with most of the rooms strung off a long hall. The first room nearest the outer door was a small bedroom with a large bed in which my brother and I slept, a chair on which we were to put our clothing rather than drop it on the floor, and, shortly after my sister's birth, her crib. From the bed I could see a hallway picture of the explosion of Vesuvius, a red horror of flames and fleeing bodies toward which I felt quite friendly when I was very young, not then knowing what it meant except bright color and lively lines. The next room off the hallway was the bathroom, all our own and a luxurious thing, with a tub, a sink, and a toilet that didn't have to be shared with neighbors. On Wednesday and Thursday nights we watched the big, vigorous carp in the tub, to be killed on Friday (when we were, unfortunately, in school) and chopped, in concert with the chopping that sounded from a dozen other kitchens, for Friday night's meal. The toilet had constantly to be pumped with a plunger to disgorge the inventive matter—spools, apple cores, a hank of wool—my brother threw in to see the water swirl and swallow, which it often didn't. The bathroom was also the torture chamber. It was here, after a long lecture explaining that the act was essential to the improvement of our conduct and we would be grateful for the lesson later on, that the strap was slowly, very slowly, pulled out of the loops on my father's pants while we bent over the lidded toilet bowl to be whipped, my brother much more often than I. He was an adventuresome explorer and breaker, while I was already well practiced in the hypocrisies of being a good girl. Furthermore, there was something shameful, except for extraordinary infractions, in beating a girl; a girl was for slapping rather than whipping.

The next room along the hallway was the kitchen where we chattered, ate, fought over who had more slices of banana in his dish and who was the biggest pig, the one who ate fast or the one who ate slowly, savoring each delicious bit when the other had long finished. Here we watched my mother peel, for our pleasure, a potato or an apple in one long unbroken coil. It was in the kitchen that we learned to understand Yiddish from my father's accounts of union news read from the socialist paper, the *Freiheit*. My mother read from the *Jewish Daily Forward* the heartbreaking stories gathered in the "Bintel Brief" (bundle of letters) that wept of abandoned wives, of "Greene Cousines," spritely immigrant girls who were hanky-pankying with the eldest sons of households, set to marry rich girls and become famous doctors. The stories moved me deeply, as all stories of betrayal and abandonment did, while my mother laughed. We loved to watch her laugh, big tears rolling down her face as the laughter rocked her plump body back and forth, but I found her humor chilling, heartless. She told one laughing story that appalled me for years: there was a man who could neither sit nor stand nor lie down (this with elaborations of voice and gesture), so he found a solution—he hanged himself. Another story concerned an old man who had trouble peeing—great effort and pain contorted her face and body—and consulted a doctor for relief. The doctor asked the man how old he was. Eighty-three. "Well," said the doctor, "you've peed enough. Go home, old man." We were constantly told to respect the old; here she was being amused by a sick old man. It wasn't until I picked up the fatalistic ironies of Jewish humor that I understood and almost forgave her the cruel jokes.

Beyond the kitchen the hallway opened to the "living room," almost always unused because we had few relatives and they visited rarely. We might look at the things in it but must not touch, except to practice the piano when that inevitable time came. The room was my mother's art museum, her collection of treasures. In the china closet a few pieces of cut glass, an etched pitcher, two little china bowls. On the round oak table a machine-embroidered cloth covered with fat red and pink roses and thick green stems with thorns; a mighty work I thought it, and so did she, since she paid the Arab peddler who sold it to her endless weekly quarters for its ebullience. On a sideboard stood my favorite piece—a marble bowl on whose rim rested two or three pigeons (a copy of a famous Roman mosaic repeated in many materials throughout the centuries). The pigeons could be lifted off and set back into little holes in the rim, a loving, absorbing game and a rare privilege never at all permitted my brother. He could not resist inventive variations on any theme, would try to place the pigeons where there were no holes and they would certainly crash, and he would get a beating and—just better not. It was in such circumstances that our parents used an odd phrase for both of us: "They have to know from where the feet grow," an amused reference to our curiosity, a phrase that my mind moved from feet to knees to genitals, where the ancient phrase with its sexual connotations probably found its origins. Not for the first or the last time I wondered why words and suggestions allowed grown-ups were forbidden children. There was no answer, it was just another example of "walking on eggs," words I found felicitous to describe our delicately balanced lives.

The end room was my parents' bedroom with its big bed, chests of drawers, and my mother's talented sewing machine. Her feet rocking the treadle that said in metal letters "Singer," her hand smoothing the material taut as the needle chased her fingers, the turning, turning spool of thread feeding the jumping needle were a stunning show. Equally remarkable were the narrow long drawers, three on each side of the machine. You pulled a knob and out came long open boxes full of papers of shining, meticulously spaced pins, empty spools to string as trains, full spools that spilled baby rainbows, bits of silk and matte cotton to mix and match in myriad combinations, the dull with the shiny, the yellow with the blue, the white with the red, the square with the round; endless. Whether it was because of the dignity of the parental bed or the multitude of treasures in the sewing machine, it was in this room that my brother and I played most peaceably, most happily, a room I still see, rain softly streaming down its windows, when I hear Mozart quartets. That end room was also the room of the fire escape. The balconies that jut out of modern apartment houses are empty stages, staring and lifeless compared with the old fire escape and its dynamic design of zigzag stairs and the teasing charm of potential danger when the metal stairs were wet with icy rain. Our fire escapes were densely inhabited by mops, short lines of washed socks, geranium plants, boxes of seltzer bottles, and occasional dramatic scenes. Skinny Molly, whose mother had an explosive temper, could escape by running down the fire-escape stairs where her fat mother couldn't follow, forcing her to expend her rage by threatening, "Wait till your father gets home, you crazy thing!" The fire escape was our viewing balcony down on the eventful lot we shared with Monterey Avenue, and it became our minute bedroom on hot nights when we slept folded on each other tight as petals on a bud, closed from the perilous stairs by a high board.

My family arrived on Lafontaine the summer before I was six and ready to be enrolled in the first grade, my brother in kindergarten. As I had learned to do in European trains and stations, in inns, on the vastness of the ship *Susquehanna* when I was an immigrant four-year-old, I studied every landmark, every turning of our new surroundings.

On the day we registered for school, P.S. 58 on Washington Avenue at 176th Street, my mother pointed out each turn, the number of blocks to the left or right and here we were at the big red building, the school, across from the little white building, the library. On the first day of school we went unaccompanied—hold his hand, don't talk to strange men. He complained that I was squeezing his hand and I probably was, tense and worried, avidly searching for the places I had marked out on our route: first to Tremont Avenue and right to the cake store, cross Third Avenue under the El, pass the butcher's with the pigs' feet in the window, cross Tremont at the bicycle shop to the barber's pole, continue on to the white library, and cross Washington Avenue to the school. It was a long walk, and I reached the school confused and exhausted, with just enough presence of mind to thrust the papers my mother had given me at the first teacher I saw, who led us to our respective rooms. We made the trip three more times that day, home for lunch and back and home again at three, and I was so bloated with triumph on the last journey that I varied the turns and crossings while my brother pulled in the directions he had memorized, as frightened as I had been that morning. With no memory of the feeling and no sympathy, I pulled him along, calling him a crybaby.

Except for those journeys, all that remains of P.S. 58 is a Mrs. Henkel, a brown old lady addicted to Spencerian handwriting. She pushed our hands around and around on the ridged, worn desks, grinding dust into our skin so that a number of us developed abscesses. Somehow the practice stopped; we were never told why. Certainly it could not have been complaints from our awed mothers, to whom schools were sacred citadels, except maybe English-speaking Mrs. Horowitz, who navigated comfortably in the alien worlds.

As the street, the shops, the people became more familiar, there were rules to learn, accumulated gradually and hardened into immutability like big pink patches always England in geography books, like Italy always the shape of a boot. Rumanian ladies used rouge and laughed a lot and ran around too much. Hungarian men were stuck-up and played cards late into the night and all day on Sunday. Bad girls who didn't go to school and who hid with tough boys were invariably the daughters of Polish janitors. Saturday night thumping and crashing and loud Victrola records came exclusively from Irish houses. The Jews stuck together, the Neapolitans and Sicilians stuck together, altogether apart from the northern Italians. Yet, in spite of momentary flare-ups, a mutter of anti-Semitism, "savage" thrown at a Sicilian, they clung to one another, arranging and rearranging the symbiotic couplings of the poor and uncomprehending in confrontations with the enemy, the outsider who spoke English without an accent. Except for a few entertaining, itinerant drunks, unaccented English was the alarm for the wary silence and the alert poise of the hunted. Not that it was a troublesome block. Most of the inhabitants were inert with timidity, but some of them had had and all of them had heard fearsome stories of brushes with truant officers, visiting nurses, people from naturalization offices, *Them* of the bewildering powers, and uncomfortably close. The Bronx County Building was stuffed with policemen, judges, immigration officials, women who looked like nurses or assistant principals. This confident, inimical enclave that spoke fast English and ate peanut butter sandwiches on white bread sat at our edge of Crotona Park, dourly in our line of vision almost everywhere we went. We children couldn't imagine them in ordinary tenements or frame houses, like ours, so we pushed them all into cold cubicles in the big-bellied building, like sides of beef in a huge butcher's icebox.

2

Forebears

As they leave few vestiges of dwelling places, not a slab of house wall standing, only subterranean caves that eat into the earth rather than vault the sky as places of worship, the ancient poor shed their ancestors, leaving them to become nameless dust when they fled plagues and famines and wars. This was particularly true of the Jews, almost constantly in flight, forced or cautionary; Jerusalem to Rome under Titus, burned out of York to settle in Lincoln, to be driven to London and expelled to wander southward where their skills were needed, and then no longer, by the Spanish kings. From Spain to Salonika, to Amsterdam, to Venice, to Lyons, to Cologne. Several centuries later, the great exodus from central Europe to America to escape conscription and pogroms and to find "ah Jahb," the first word in most immigrant vocabularies. They dragged their large down puffs like fat clouds, their burnished samovars, the candlesticks and hand-embroidered cloths for the Sabbath table, the old men their prayer shawls, the women their *shaytlin* (wigs worn by married women) and cotton headcloths and slips of paper supplied by

HIAS, the guardians of the Golden Gates, whose formal name, rarely used, was Hebrew Immigrant Aid Society.

They brought with them Moses, Esther, Abraham, Isaac, Joseph, Sarah, David, Solomon, miracle rabbis, and old stories gentle, magical, and bawdy. But, as if they could carry no more baggage, they left their closer ancestors in a thousand scattered cemeteries from which a few vivid flowers grew, to be pressed by each family in its Old Country book. There were few who did not have, somewhere among their ancestors, a bride so beautiful that she was strewn with rose petals on her way to the *chuppa* (the bridal canopy), her dainty little feet lightly treading the red velvet rug that was her path. As she shone under the canopy, one despairing young man ran from the happy crowd to drown himself in the nearby river. Another went home to develop brain fever, struggling with the Angel of Death for months and never the same again. When Zuleika Dobson appeared in my life, she, too, stood pink-cheeked and glittering under a canopy while young men in side locks languished and fell before her. Another graveyard flower was an ancestral rabbi of unerring wisdom who knew how to rekosher an unkoshered pot, how to frighten the tongue of a lying shrew, and who, at least once, had exorcised a dybbuk.

My family was unfortunately free of these engaging ghosts, no learned Gaon, no village Esther. My parents were skeptics and, bored with the spates of *bubbe meises* (grandmother's tales), preferred to tell pointed little stories about each other's relatives. My earliest known ancestor was my mother's grandmother, Kaila, for whom I was named. All I know about her is that she was an entertaining grandmother and the wise woman of her Warsaw ghetto street, the Tvarda Gass, where I was born. My mother's father—I think he was Kaila's son, but I'm not sure—was a tinsmith, a quiet, passive man who died early, after falling off a roof on which he was working. He left twelve children—a thirteenth had been smothered in infancy lying between its sleeping parents, a not uncommon incident. Most of the children, like my mother, had one year's schooling, from the age of seven to eight, and then went out to work, running errands, moving barrels and sacks in markets, selling shoelaces and buttonhooks, sweeping up the floors of dressmaking establishments, each learning enough to progress into an apprenticeship and a better-paying job. The youngest girls stayed at home to help my grandmother. About her I know singularly little except that she was religious, apparently colorless, and possibly not overly bright. My mother, a gifted raconteur and mimic, rarely spoke of her, in itself a strange fact, and stranger still since it was in her house that I spent my earliest years and it was in her house that my brother was born. We have pictures of two young aunts, arms around each other's shoulders, a coquettish silk rose on one bosom, a swirl of black hair on the other's head, winsome, girlish half-smiles fixed as their immortality. There are no other pictures, an effect of poverty or superstition that might have been a lingering whisper of the biblical injunction against graven images.

The exodus from the Warsaw ghetto that brought us to America took three aunts to Buenos Aires, one uncle to Paris, another to London. I have made sporadic efforts to locate them, with no success. The only relative on my mother's side whom I actually met was a cousin, chic and multilingual, a functionary with the Free Polish in England and married to an Englishman. I've lost her, too, as I've lost a large number of unknown relatives of two or three generations destroyed in the Warsaw ghetto. From what little I know of some of them, the spirited, the courageous, they might have taken part in the ghetto uprising. I don't know, I hope.

My paternal ancestors are much more vivid, brought to life largely by the quick eye and tongue of my mother. Perhaps the best way to introduce them is in the person of my father just arrived on Ellis Island.

Having installed my pregnant mother and my one-year-old self in the flat of my grandmother and my young aunts with the promise that he would send for us soon, he went off to America. He arrived an unencumbered princeling, twenty-six and handsome, with fine shirts and handmade shoes in his real leather valise, no peasant bundle of sentimental odds and ends to embarrass him, no pink-eyed crusty-headed child to threaten his entry. He had an uncle's promise of a bed and an introduction to a "landsman" whose occupation was sniffing out jobs. And he had the freedom to taste girls again. It would be as easy as picking flowers in a summer field, the white candid daisies, the yellow buttercups peering out of the grass, the round pink clover, all the little "Greene Cousines." Their song, one of the most famous among the many immigrant songs, described their teeth as matched pearls, their eyes as doves, their cheeks as pomegranates; their feet never walked, they skipped and danced. They were optimistic and courageous; a new life meant several kinds of new life, free of the frowning bearded father worlds away, the mumbling scowling aunts erased. It was not my father's habit to pursue; he stood grand and unsmiling while the pomegranate girls in their starched shirtwaists and pearly buttoned shoes did him obeisance, and a few, to use the lovely chivalric euphemism, "did him solace." A highly skilled craftsman who could make the whole sample shoe, decorations and all, to be shown to a Fifth Avenue buyer, my father got a job quickly. He moved out of the niche in a wall in his old uncle's railroad flat and found a younger, more raffish family who provided a room, robust Polish-Jewish meals, and the company of several spirited boarders. It took almost three years to bring us to America. World War I was drawing to a close but still tearing Poland apart: communications were erratic; Warsaw, dismembered by Germany and Russia, was a corpse. Yet, knowing something of my father's upbringing and vanity, I suspect that caused him little concern or disappointment.

He was a royal baby, his birth a gift of immortality. He was a miracle, a sudden kindling of cold ashes stirred by God's hand. All privilege was his. Year after year my grandmother had produced girls and only girls, a few stillborn, one or two victims of diphtheria or scarlet fever, but five or six thriving as big, marriageable maidens. The menopause years were approaching while my embittered grandmother muttered over the *cholent* (a stew of potatoes, carrots, meat, and prunes) that she shoved into the oven on Friday afternoons to cook slowly through the night and provide a warm meal on Saturday when no stove might be lit. She mumbled angrily while she ironed, spitting the dampening water as if it were venom. Someone, maybe an old witch who envied her her good house, her gold watch, her silky new *shaytl*, had cursed her with the Evil Eye, depriving her of a son, a *Kaddish* to pray for her after her death. The girls' prayers, if they prayed at all, counted for nothing; like animals, they had no souls and no voices to God's ear. My grandfather was indifferent to the whole matter, heartily sick of the Evil Eye and the sacrificial fasts his wife imposed on herself and him, when he allowed it. He was impatient with her charities, which involved her in quarrels with other women about what orphan should or should not be given a wedding dress and a dowry, and impatient with the superstitions among which she moved fearfully. He enjoyed the noisy gaggle of girls who racketed around in his house as he enjoyed being the most important Jew in his village near Lodz. When the manager of the big tobacco factory, the principal source of local employment, died, my grandfather was moved up from foreman, an almost incredible appointment for a Jew, and he earned enough to buy his rangy house and feed the girls as well as a number of orphans and any traveling Jew who was far from home during the holidays. He was curious and gregarious and handed out cigarettes and advice with broad profligacy; a lovable man, my mother said, in spite of the fact that he reeked of tobacco, and under his light and sometimes foolish quips—just to keep the talk going—a smart man.

Several of my aunts grew into marriage and brought their young husbands to the house. One opened a dry-goods store with help from my grandfather, another was given a job in the tobacco factory, a third was a scholar, required to do nothing but study and be an honor to the family. As my aunt, Teibele, the Little Dove, grew rounder and rounder with pregnancy, my grandmother grew thinner and more dour; her bleeding had stopped, the menopause had taken her, sterile of sons. Teibele's baby was born, thank God a girl, and Grandma began to look a little better, her cheeks less gray, her back straighter, a belly pushing out between the lean hips. The belly ultimately became my father and my grandmother's ecstasy. No infant was ever so brave at his circumcision, no baby so quick to walk and speak, never a child so beautiful as her Yukele. The house and everything in it belonged to her miracle. She awoke each morning at four-thirty to listen for the baker's wagon and raced down the stairs to greet him as he dropped the sack of bread and rolls at the back door. She carefully examined each roll, rejecting those not quite baked enough, those too well baked; squeezed each for the proper mixture of resilience and softness, took the best three or four, went back upstairs to put them under her pillow to save for her little King David, and went back to sleep. At dinner, eight or ten adults, a couple of adolescents, a few younger children at table, no one made a gesture, not even Grandpa, toward the platters of chicken and boiled beef until Yukele, from his infancy to his early manhood, had made his choice.

My father's shirts, cut of Paris silks, were made by a Warsaw shirtmaker. The local cobbler would do for the rest of the family, but my father's shoes were made to measure by the best establishment in the capital. There was talk of sending him to a yeshiva in Warsaw, where he might pick up a little Russian or German as well as Talmud and Gemorrah. Grandma wouldn't have it and insisted that he be tutored at home. My philosophical grandfather agreed. (Suddenly it seems dreadful that I do not know his first name or that of my other Old Country relatives or what they looked like except for the slanging little contests of wit and malice between my parents. He spoke of my mother's family as *knaydlach*, round dumplings, all fat cheek and ass and no neck. My mother spoke of his favorite sister, a tall lissome beauty according to him, as a board with a hole. He said she had a vulgar Warsaw mouth; she said he spoke like a coarse provincial drover, the most foulmouthed of Jews. And so on, while we listened, entranced, silent, hardly breathing, our backs bent hard with the feigned virtue of homework. It is still not possible, and probably never will be, for me to see Picasso's flat wooden women without hearing my mother's laughing voice, *"A brate mit a loch."*)

Having agreed that Yukele could stay at home, Grandpa insisted that he learn a trade as well. Sulking, wailing, shrieking that the silken hands must not be defiled, while Grandpa hummed happy little songs about merry tailors and lusty drovers, my grandmother reluctantly accepted this commonplace for her golden son. At twenty, my father was ready for a bigger world. He was a fast reckoner, read and wrote Yiddish and Polish well, and could follow Hebrew prayers and texts competently, all my carefree grandfather asked for. Pitifully little for my grandmother, who wanted a radiant rabbi with the beard of Abraham and the side locks of David, the wisdom of Solomon and the enlightenment of Maimonides, and—even if he was a heinous apostate—Spinoza's renown among learned *goyim*. The actual spur, according to the meager, somewhat apocryphal family history, that sent my father into an apprenticeship with a skilled cobbler in Warsaw was my mother. He, when he was fond of her, romanticized their meeting—a wedding where he watched her dance, a gathering of young people where she sang and played the mandolin. She insisted that their meeting was forced on her by her mother, who had begun to speak of her as "already a girl in the years" (she was twenty-two or twenty-three) and had enlisted a matchmaker who also had dealings with my grandfather. He was beginning to sicken with cancer of the lungs and was eager to see his spoiled son under the control of a competent girl before he died.

It was a lackluster courtship. My father pursued casually, on instructions from the matchmaker and the urging of his father. My mother eluded, without a touch of maidenly coyness. She was earning well, helping to support her younger siblings from the proceeds of her own corset shop. She enjoyed not only the independence but also the fun of making a lace-trimmed black corset with a tight waist for the mistress of a banker. She liked talking and joking and listening to the confidences of the prettiest *shiksas* around town, invariably referred to by my father as "prostitutkes," which was invariably countered by my mother with a reference to one of his idiot cousins who had willingly spread for a saddler, the price a glass ring.

My mother mentioned it once and only once, as part of a lecture on female independence and the overrated charms of marriage, that she was in love with a Gentile for a number of years and for that reason thoroughly resistant to all marriage offers, several from prosperous businessmen to whom an appealing, playful girl with a good business head was markedly attractive. The love story was left there; no continuation, no end. One can assume that the anticipated shock and pain of a mixed marriage to both families, sharpened by the notorious anti-Semitism of the Polish and the fear of Poles in every Jew, forced the ultimate separation.

The desultory courtship went on while my father developed fine skills and a keen eye for the English suits in elegant shop windows, while my mother's business flourished and her rounds of songs and mazurkas widened, often with *goy* friends, a shame for the neighbors, my grandmother complained. My paternal grandmother had heard about this, too—the grapevine among Jewish communities was as dense a meshwork as Renaissance politics—and greeted my mother on her first visit with her eyes firmly cast down. To look at her would have been to burn her up, this *shiksa* with the Polish name (Lonia Babicz) who worked and collected money on the Sabbath and had declared that she would never wear a *shaytl*. The grandfather addressed her with courtliness, conducted her to the best chair, said that he had heard it was becoming the fashion for women to smoke in Warsaw, would she care for a cigarette? He admired her pretty dress and how small her feet were and continued to seduce her for his son. She married the son, my mother said, because she loved the father. His unremitting flattery was entertaining but nothing more. It was his patience with his dotty wife, the inventive games he played with his grandchildren, the courage that hid his pain, his generous interest in everyone, and the love that shone on her like the sun that made her accede to his delicately expressed dying wish. She married his Yukele shortly before her old true love died.

I was born a year later. The year after that my father left for America. It should have been a happy infancy, dandled and sung to by young aunts, near my mother, who worked at home after her shop was confiscated with the outbreak of war. Among the few Polish words I remember are references to me as "a pretty doll"; obviously I didn't lack attention. But I missed my father and looked for him constantly, behind doors, under tables, in the street. I was told that he was in a place where everything was good and where we would soon go. If a toy broke, he would buy me another, a better one, when we got to America. If there was

no sugar to put in my milk, I would have lots of sugar, heaps as
tall as trees, in America. As wartime supplies of food diminished
to coarse bread and potatoes, my life was filled with images of
raisins and chocolate, cookies and dolls, white slippers and pink
hair bows, all waiting for me in a big box called America, which
would be mine soon, very soon.

3

Voyage and Discovery

When my brother was born, I was eighteen months old. My father, for whom I was still searching, had been in New York for six months. Our Warsaw apartment turned dark, the singing stopped. It need hardly be said that I was jealous, felt abandoned, unloved, coldly shadowed while the full warm light that was mine now circled him. It cannot have been that my grandmother and aunts and mother suddenly stopped loving me, and I might in time have grown interested in him, beginning with the gallant way he peed, upward in a little shining arch, out of a finger in a peculiar place. But he was a very sick child and the household alternated between sad, quiet staring and frantic dashing to rescue him from death. His head was bright, alert, and very large compared to the arms and legs that would not develop beyond thin, boneless ropes. He was a classic picture of the rachitic famine child who still tears the heart of the newspaper reader, the television viewer. We were not too poor to buy the food he needed; it was simply unavailable, grabbed up by the military for its soldiers. My mother took the baby from doctor to doctor, all of whom gave her the same short answer: "All this child needs is a steady, normal diet." Because her food intake was meager, the milk she gave him was insufficient; my aunts scoured the city, offering large sums for an orange or two, an egg, a pint of milk, with no success. I grew thin and listless.

The last doctor my mother saw in Warsaw, made blunt by the misery he could not remedy, shouted at her, "Leave the boy, he's going to die anyway. Take the girl to America while there's still time. Or do you want to sit with two dead children in this graveyard city?"

We left for America. My brother was two and a half, a babbler in several languages, a driven entertainer and flirt. His arms and hands were weak but usable, his legs not at all; he moved with amazing, mischievous rapidity by shuffling on his behind when he wasn't being carried. I was four, grown silent and very capable. I could lift him to the pot, clean him, and take him off. I could carry him to bed and mash his potato. I knew where he might bump his head, where he might topple, how to divert him when he began to blubber. It was a short childhood. I had my first baby at not quite four, better trained in maternal wariness and responsibility than many fully grown women I later observed. At four I also knew one could intensely love and as intensely hate the being who was both core and pit of one's life.

The month-long journey across devastated Europe to reach our ship, the *Susquehanna*, in Rotterdam remains with me as snatches of dream. I am sitting with my brother on my lap, in a room full of heavy dark furniture that I have never seen before. I am telling him that our mother went to buy food and will be back soon. I hope that she will come back, but I'm not sure; over and over, in every dark dream, I am not sure. I don't say this to him but wonder what I will do, where we will go, if she doesn't come back, as our father didn't. I continue to talk to him. We'll soon be on another choo-choo train and then the big, big ship that will take us to our father in America. He is silent in these dreams, his face old, serious, as if he were listening to the fears under my bright optimistic patter.

The next vision is actual recollection: a long cobbled quay marching into a world of water, more water than I had ever imagined. On the side of the quay a stall at which a woman shining with smiles and sweat stands frying small cakes. My mother buys three and hands me one. I expect it to be sweet and it tastes like fish. The vomit leaps out of my mouth, down my clean dress, and into the cracks around the cobblestones. What do they do in this place to girls who vomit on their streets? Will they keep me off their ship? The pink sweaty lady washes it away with a bucket of water. My mother thanks her in the Dutch she has picked up, I say my best Polish thank you, my smarty brother dazzles her with a *"Merci beaucoup"* someone had taught him on a train, and we go to look for the *Susquehanna*, my mother carrying my brother and one big valise and I two big bundles.

Just as I find it a great loss not to know my grandparents' first names, I feel deprived of what should have been an unforgettable sight: the big ship as it swayed on the waterfront and, later, the endless corridors, the stairs, the crowds of people, the disorder, the shouting, the weeping in terror, in relief, in joy, that my mother described. We were on the ship a full month, listed in steerage. I don't know where my brother and I actually stayed, however. As if our lives were designed to fill every requirement of the classic immigrant hegira, typhus raged through steerage, my exhausted mother one of the victims. We children must have been taken care of in some other part of the ship by strangers whom I cannot remember except as sensations of pleasure: an India rubber ball whose lovely colors played hide and seek with each other and the man who gave it to me, a slight man in a brown hat who limped. I searched for him for years after. A slight man in a brown hat who limped was the dream lover of my adolescence, a steady image through the short, searing crushes, the unbuttoned blouse and the frightened crawl of boys' fingers.

Knowing that there would be a long wait at Ellis Island, my father had equipped himself with a couple of Hershey bars to nibble on, and when he finally picked me up to kiss me, I tasted the chocolate and announced to my mother, "Our father has a sweet mouth." It was frequently quoted as an example of my dainty, feminine grace, and only four years old, mind you. I have often thought it was an act of propitiation: I am eager to love you; love me, please.

At Ellis Island we were questioned and examined by immigration officials and told our English names. Because my Polish birth certificate said "Jew-child Carolina" I was dubbed and registered as "Caroline," a barbed-wire fence that divided me from myself throughout my school years. I hated it and would never answer my father when he tried to be fancy and American in public, addressing me by a name that belonged entirely to P.S. 58, P.S. 57, P.S. 59, to Theodore Roosevelt High School, to James Monroe High School, to Hunter College, not to me. How we got to Kate I don't know. My mother must have sought it out to keep as clear as possible the link to her grandmother Kaila, not realizing how intensely Catholic a name it then was. Being serenaded as "K-K-K-Katy, my beautiful Katy" was a flattering bewilderment until I realized it was not written for me and then grew bored and irritated with the repetition from elderly relatives. (As bored as I later became with their descendants and their witty greeting, "Kiss me, Kate.") My brother, the master mimic, learned "K-K-K-Katy" immediately and learned, too—our weaponry of injuries that were deep and yet unpunishable was uncannily sophisticated—how much it annoyed me, and he sang it constantly to the admiration of the old uncles and aunts who never ceased to wonder at the speed with which he picked up English songs and the pretty, true voice on which they floated clear, loud, and incessant.

Instead of a city of silver rivers and golden bridges, America turned out to be Uncle David's flat on Avenue C in which my father had first lived when he came to America. We walked up several flights of dark stairs and knocked on a door pasted over with glazed patterned paper of connecting rectangles and circles in blue and red and green, whose lines I liked to trace with my eye while the others talked. That door led to a large kitchen with a round table in the center, a few chairs around it, and, off to a side, a brown wooden icebox. At another side, a shining black stove whose cooking lids were lifted by a clever long black hook when pieces of coal had to be added to the waning fire. From the kitchen ran a narrow dark alley with divisions that made niches for beds and then opened into a small living room at whose end there were two windows with views of clouds and chimneys. Only once were we held to look down to the street below; never were we to try on our own, and we couldn't, so thoroughly were we watched by our entranced Uncle David, who looked like God and Moses and, more often, Old King Cole. He had a long white beard and puffs of white hair leaping from the edge of his skullcap and a magical skill of putting his finger inside his cheek and pulling it out to make a big popping sound. He laughed a lot, told incomprehensible stories about Italians whose only English was "sonnomabitz," drank great quantities of tea, sipped from a saucer and drained through a cube of sugar held in his teeth. Everything about him was wonderful: the black straps and boxes he wrapped on his arms and forehead and the rhythmic bowing of his prayers when he was God; the fluttering old fingers and light touch of his gray carpet slippers as he paced a Chassidic dance when he was Old King Cole.

The rest of his household consisted of two middle-aged spinster daughters. Rachel was a plump, bustling, talkative woman who addressed us as her little sheep, which made us feel pathetic and affecting and sure we could get anything out of her—another candy and yet another—and we played her. In spite of her bounty and mushy vulnerability, I was afraid of her. She wore glasses so thick that her eyes were invisible behind concentric circles of shine. Though her cheeks were high-colored and her teeth strong and yellow, she looked like a mechanical woman, a machine with flashing, glassy circles for eyes. The third member of the household was completely apart from us and truly fearsome. Yentel (a name, I was later told, that derived from the Italian "Gentile") was tall and gaunt, blind and deaf. She moved through the small apartment deftly, measuring her spaces with long, constantly moving fingers. She made the beds, pulling, smoothing, lining up the edges with her subtle, restless fingers. She shelled peas, she peeled potatoes and plucked chickens. While my brother sang and shuffled around Rachel and Uncle David, I watched her out of the corner of my eye. I didn't know what blind really meant; anyone who was so dextrous could not be entirely without vision and I was afraid she would see me staring at her if I watched her with my eyes wide open.

Though I was relieved of some of the care of my brother, I still had to be in charge many times. Uncle David and Rachel could keep him from banging into Yentel and would prepare his food, but we had confusing language difficulties that I had to unsnarl when my parents went out, my mother wildly eager to see everything and now, particularly while she had such devoted baby-sitters. My brother and I spoke Polish, Uncle David and Rachel had been brought up in Yiddish with a few Polish words they no longer remembered accurately. When my brother sleepily mumbled "*Spatch* [sleep]" they briskly rushed him to the cold toilet in the hall, vaguely remembering a similar Polish word that they thought meant shit, *sratch*. Unable to explain, I resorted to rough pantomime: run into the toilet, shake my head vigorously, pull him, confused and weeping, off the seat, and carry him to one of the beds, where I dump him and his lush glorious howling, to let them take care of the rest. Conversely I had to watch for the suffused worried face and the shifting buttocks that they tried to settle in bed while he yearned for a toilet. The story of bed and toilet was frequently told in our household to considerable laughter; my brother and I were never amused, it gave us both anxious bellyaches.

Force-fed like a Strasbourg goose by everyone who looked at him, my brother began to strengthen and even to take a few tentative steps now and then. An early talker, his only strengths his brain and speech, he was prodigious at three. He might easily have learned to read but he preferred talk, preferably oratory. The first time we were taken out on a sled one winter afternoon, he declared when we came home that so small a child (as he) must not be taken out in snowy cold. People had to realize that a small body got colder faster, that snow was for animals with fur and not for people with skins. And so on and so on, in his adept combination of splashing guilt as he charmed. And how he could cry, high wide luxuriant wails to which his whole body danced, and to which everyone responded anxiously, except one time when we were taken on an elevated train and, at one station, a black man walked in and sat opposite us. I didn't know how to feel: maybe he was a charred man, darkened like wood in a fire and I must be sorry for him, maybe he ate coal, maybe he was some sort of monkey like those in a picture book and I should be afraid of him. While sorting it out, I admired the light palms of his hands against the dark backs, the big purple lips, and the wide holes in his nose. My brother shrieked in terror, screaming—in Polish, fortunately—"Take him away, take that black giant away! He's going to eat me! Kill him, Papa, kill him!" It was a crowded train; to give up our seats and move to stand in another car would have been foolish. My father slapped the small pointing finger and with his hand stifled the howling. The child thrust his head into my mother's armpit and, shuddering, rode that way the rest of the journey.

My brother's fear of blacks dispelled itself in the stellar entertainment we found on 98th Street, between Lexington and Third avenues where we had moved from the Lower East Side. At the top of the street there were three tall-stooped narrow tenements and below, running to Third, small houses with crooked porches. These were black houses and to us places of great joy and freedom. My brother was already walking quite well and we were allowed the street—I was always to hold his hand and watch that he didn't go into the gutter and see that he didn't get dirty and not to talk to strange men and not wander around the corner. We watched, at a distance, the black children fly in and out of their houses, calling strange sounds, bumping, pummeling, rolling, leaping, an enchantment of "wild beasts" my father never permitted us to be. The best of the lower street were the times when everyone, adults and children, marched up and down, carrying bright banners, and to the sound of trumpets and drums sang, "Ohlly Nohly, Ohlly Nooo. Bumpera bumpera bump bump bum, Ohlly Noooo." Ohlly Nohly became our favorite rainy-day game, my brother banging on a pot with a clothespin, I tootling through tissue paper on a comb, high-stepping jauntily, roaring from hallway to kitchen to bedroom our version of a revival hymn that must have begun with "Holy Lord, Oh Holy Lord." We never could reconstruct the bumpera bumpera words though we never forgot the tune.

It was on 98th Street, across from the tall long sinister stone wall on which the Third Avenue El trains came to rest, that I began to know I would never get to America. Though I learned in the kindergarten on 96th Street, among the many other English words that I taught my brother with a prissy, powerful passion, that I lived in America, it was not the America promised me in Warsaw or by the chocolate sweetness of my father's mouth. There were no sacks of candy and cookies, no dolls, no perennial summer that meant America. America was a stern man whose duty it was to cure us of being the cosseted spoiled little beasts our mother and her idiot sisters had allowed to flourish. At the far remove of decades, I can understand how infuriating it was for this indulged semibachelor to be saddled with a wife and two noisy children whom he hadn't the courage to abandon nor the wish to live with. Nothing to do but mold us with speed and force into absolute obedience, to make his world more tolerable and, I often suspected, to avenge himself on us for existing.

It was his habit to take a constitutional after dinner every night, a health measure he clung to all his life, as he clung to the bowel-health properties of the cooked prunes he ate every morning. One autumn twilight, when my brother was about four and I five and a half, we walked down 98th Street, toward Third Avenue, I averting my eyes from the tall black wall that deadened the other side of the street. Somewhere on Third Avenue we slowed at a row of shops, one of them a glory of brilliantly lit toys. Carefully, deliciously, my brother and I made our choices. He wanted the boat with big white sails to float in the bathtub or maybe the long line of trains that ran on tracks or maybe the red fire engine with a bell. I chose a big doll whose eyes opened and closed and a house with tiny beds and chairs and a clothes wringer in the kitchen. Or, maybe, the double pencil box crammed with coloring pencils, serious school pencils, a pen holder, and three pen points. As my brother lilted on in gay covetousness, the wariness that was already as much a part of me as blue eyes and wild blond hair made me suddenly turn. It was night. There was no mother, no father, on the dark street and I didn't know where we were. Feeling my fear, my brother turned, too, and began to cry heartbreakingly—no imperious shrieks for attention now, this was deep sorrow, the sorrow of the lost and abandoned. I felt, too, the cold skinlessness, the utter helplessness, the sickness of betrayal. I wanted to cry but I must not. As in the heavy rooms of my later dreams, as on the ship when we were separated from our sick mother, I told him not to worry, I would take care of him. Look—I wasn't afraid, I wasn't crying. By the time—and I cannot possibly estimate its length because the overwhelming fear and the effort to control it filled all dimensions— my mother burst out of a doorway to run to us, I had become, in some corner of my being, an old woman. It didn't matter that she hugged and kissed us and that my father carefully explained that it was merely a lesson to teach us to walk with him and not linger. I held them to be bad strangers and would not talk to either for days.

My brother sloughed off the incident, as he did many others; I remembered and judged, accumulating a sort of Domesday Book on my father's deeds. He sensed and feared it, and it was that fear on which I battened, the tears he could not make me shed freezing as an icy wall between us.

4

Fifth Floor

Our fifth-floor landing resembled in mood the *castellare* of old Italian towns, a cluster of dwellings capable of closing itself off as a fortress against invasion; no one passed our doors or walked our stairs to the roof without our knowledge and consent. We four families were thus somewhat isolated from the hamlet of 2029, special people, and as frequently happens with the isolated and special, we became a close tribe.

One of the neighbors on our landing was Fannie Herman, a skinny little sparrow, hopping, restless, a bewildered child in a strange room. Attached to the nervous spareness were large red hands and enormous bunioned feet, almost always bare. I became clearly aware of her—before that she had been, like most adults, an object in my landscape, like trees and street lamps—when I heard my mother speaking to her on the landing, in Yiddish and as to a child: "Fannie, the holidays are coming soon. Let's clean your house, you and I together. Buy a broom and a scrubbing brush for the floors and lemon oil for the furniture. I'll give you some rags. We'll wipe off the dust and sweep away the feathers.

We'll make it nice, you'll see." I had come out of our apartment and could see Fannie's meager face sharpen in terror. "Where will I buy? They talk English in the hardware store. I can't." "All right, Fannie, don't worry. Give me the money and I'll buy."

Fannie rarely went out; the street was Gehenna. She had seen her first child, a little boy, smashed by a truck on the street. Her daughters ran wild and howled on the street, the street was where Mr. Herman's car shone and lured his girls away from their homework and piano practice. Like his wife, Mr. Herman was illiterate, but under his lumbering silence, my father said, there were courage and shrewdness. In a community of factory workers he was an entrepreneur, the owner of a small kosher slaughterhouse. More amazingly, he owned, drove, and washed a car like an American. It was he who ordered the milk to be delivered, bought the children their shoes and winter coats, and supplied the bread and chickens they ate each night.

Their night meal was a fairy ritual, incomprehensible, exotic, anarchic, very seductive to the child of a reasonably well-ordered household prickly with rules. Since the Hermans' day started at dawn, the children were shooed off to bed early in the evening, long before the rest of us were, and were asleep when their father arrived carrying two paper bags, one full of large rolls, the other wrapped around a headless chicken, eviscerated but still feathered. Without a greeting, he put the bags on the kitchen table, took off his cap and coat, and put a record of cantorial music on the Victrola in the next room. Fanny set herself firmly, purposefully, on a kitchen chair, and tucking the chicken into her lap, began to pluck it with impassioned speed, her thin arm like a fast piston. The feathers soared up and spiraled down to the floor, rocked and floated into the air and onto the table, little pinfeathers danced toward the sink where they settled, quivering like winged dandelion seeds. Fannie then took the chicken to the stove where she turned and turned it over an open flame to burn off remaining stubble. The smell was fatty and bitter, as satisfying as hot tar; the smell of incantations.

Singed and stippled, the chicken was dropped into a large pot of salted boiling water. There was none of the usual busyness of preparing a table, no place settings, no napkins, no plates, no tablecloth, nothing but the bag of rolls and a feather or two. Fannie kept poking impatiently at the chicken while Mr. Herman changed the records on his Victrola, from melancholy Hebrew liturgy to melancholy Yiddish folk songs. When Fannie decided the chicken was done, she scurried toward the children's bedroom shouting, "Come eat!" The sleepy baby drooped in his high chair while the two girls in their underclothes (nightgowns were worn only by Lillian Gish) became quickly alert and plunged into the rolls, chewing them in big-cheeked mouthfuls while the chicken cooled in its pot on the table. Fannie poured off some of the soup for the next day's lunch and then, adroitly, marvelously, the chicken was torn apart. Fannie was first, plunging two fingers into the pot to pull out a wing for her baby, her miraculous resurrection of the dead boy. Then it was the father's turn; with a quick twist he had a leg and thigh. The practiced hands of the girls plucked out shreds of breast in the smooth, steady rhythm of picking buttercups in the park. There was no conversation; the only sounds were the chewing and the ululations of Yosele Rosenblatt from the Victrola. When the chicken and rolls were finished, the children went back to bed, their mouths and hands still silky with chicken fat. Fannie then fished for her own dinner—a back, a gizzard, a foot, the neck bones to suck, standing over the pot when everyone else had finished, in the habit of most of the neighborhood women. It was hard for me to leave, though it would soon be my bedtime, but Mr. Herman gave me his sign, pulling his suspenders off his shoulders, getting ready for bed. I shuffled through the feathers, scraped a few off my shoes at the door, and crossed the landing to "wash your hands," "clean your teeth."

Miriam Herman was a quiet, neat child who read library books and did her homework promptly. She was the same age as my brother and was his playmate until he decided at seven never again to play with girls, who were more disgusting than snot. Her older sister, Tobie, was my age, a gangling, rawboned girl, tall like her father, skinny and jumpy like her mother. She was taut with belligerence, her very presence threatening. Rarely admitted to jump-rope games, she would kick at a rope in its snapping rounds to trip a jumper. She would stoop suddenly, and with the big hand of her mother, grab two marbles from the games of boys who protested but were too afraid to counterattack. Some of the Jewish women said she had a "*gilgul*," a troublesome imp, in her. Others dismissed her as a "wild beast." Tobie should have hated me more actively than she did as the paragon of the prime neighborhood virtues. I practiced the piano, I was never fresh to my mother or father, I took care of my brother and baby sister (I was, in short, a coward), and Fannie kept shouting my praises at her wayward daughter, who wiped me off her earth, circling me as if I were a stump. The wrath she might have turned on me thundered around her mother instead.

The high dramas between Fannie and Tobie that pierced the Herman door and shot into the hallway mounted to frenzy when Tobie was left back in school while I skipped a class and, shortly after, won a bronze medal in a music contest. Fannie had insisted that like me—like Ruthie, like Rosie, like Sarah, like Beckie, et al—Tobie must learn to play the piano. Good-natured and afflu-ent Mr. Herman bought a piano, a baby grand, one of the wonders of our lives. Miriam practiced but Tobie could no more be tamed to music than to spelling or arithmetic. She kept on running and kicking, her long stick legs clattering down the five flights of stairs and onto the sidewalk to kick balls, cats, garbage pails; her only pauses of quiet were the minutes she sat in her father's car waiting for him to take her for a ride. The conflict between the piano and the car became a monumental struggle. Having satisfied Fannie with a baby grand, Mr. Herman cared little how and when it was used. He didn't work on the Sabbath but he wasn't particularly observant since no one had bothered to teach him the elaborate rules. So, on Saturday mornings while the prayers of downstairs Mr. Liebowitz crackled out his window, Mr. Herman drove his car around the neighboring streets, and when he grew lonely, called for his girls. Miriam had usually finished her practicing, Tobie hadn't started and wouldn't. When the auto horn sounded its signal, Fannie ran to bar the door. Tobie was not to go before she finished practicing. The girl, taller and strong with rage, tore the door open, and leaning long-necked and poisonous toward her mother, like a snake about to spit, yelled, "Crazy mother! Teeny mother! Teeny, crazy mother with the big feet! Teeny mother with the big bunions! Crazy mother with the big ugly bunion feet!" continuing the howling litany as she rocketed down the stairs. Fannie dashed back to the street window of her flat, flung it open, and screamed her spate of curses to the street and the heavens. "May the piankele be buried in the earth! May the machinkele be swallowed by the earth! May black cholera carry off both the piankele and the machinkele! May they suffer of boils! May they succumb to a dark fate!" until my mother stopped her, reminding her that she would soon have to nurse her baby and she didn't want to sour her milk, did she.

The next day Fannie would be extraordinarily subdued. She was afraid, she had cursed and would be cursed. It was on those days that an unexpected breeze, a touch that lifted the hem of a curtain, would bring her weeping to our door, the baby in her arms. The Angel of Death had flown in! And then the rocking chair had begun to rock itself! The Angel of Death was sitting in it, sitting and waiting! He was waiting to grab her baby as he had grabbed her other boy. My mother took her back after a while to her own apartment, explaining a breeze, a careless push against a rocker. Reason worked but never for long. Though she trusted my mother almost slavishly, the Angel of Death was closer to Fannie, possibly her most intimate relation.

It might have been because I felt banished by my mother's absorption with my new baby sister—no time to make me a new pongee sailor dress, no time to hear me sing "Over the Hill" with heartbreaking quavers—that I spent more and more time with Fannie. I told her about the stories I read and complained about my teachers; sometimes I played a sad Chopin waltz on her baby grand. She told me in Yiddish and her few English words of her childhood. She was orphaned at six in a small Polish town and taken into a big house as the most minor servant whose job it was to scrub all the outside stairs in all weathers. Her bed was a pile of sacks in the cellar and her food was bread and a potato or apple she stole from the cellar bins. Mr. Herman was a stable boy for the same house, also an orphan, so they got married. It was an awful story to me—the imagined cold, the imagined hunger—like a story of starvelings in Grimm. But she spoke without anger or sadness; these were her facts, neither just nor unjust.

One late holiday afternoon, while her baby was sleeping and Miriam and Tobie were out for an auto ride, Fannie said to me, words and hands mumbling, "You know, Katie, you know what I want more than anything, except my children should be healthy? I would like to know how to write my name." She couldn't find a pencil or paper but there was the great expanse of the dusty piano. Guiding her finger, I traced with her "Fannie, Fannie, Fannie," countless times through the wide gray space. She was enchanted and indefatigable. From time to time I did try her with a pencil on paper but her hand was too awkward for the small, tight movements. She became discouraged, bleakly defeated. So back to new accumulations of dust on the piano, on the big unused dining table, on the chests of drawers. Best, when the frosts came, was melting her name into the icy windows, her finger skating along fairly briskly without my help. When she had traced "Fannie" in dust and frost thousands of times, I suggested "Herman." No success at all, she wouldn't even try. When I asked her why not, she looked at me worriedly and said after a long silence, "It's his name and I don't know my own other one. So maybe Fannie is enough." I tried "Herman" again and she tried a bit to please me but it went poorly.

I had to spend more time with our new baby when my mother began to work at selling corsets from door to door in the late afternoons, and my father complained I wasn't practicing enough. There was talk of moving out of Lafontaine Avenue and ultimately we did. I don't know if Fannie ever wrote her name again, although I liked for a long time to picture her, and still do, etching the dust with her forefinger, curve after careful curve.

The Haskells lived next door to the Hermans. He rarely spoke, which didn't matter (we children rarely connected with the men, the voices that filled our world were those of women, the Mothers, large stoves to warm at, sofas to read on, home base, an apple after school), but he did have one godlike gesture. He and his wife, whom I liked to look at because she resembled a melting vanilla cone, had no children and spent much of their Sundays reading the Sunday *American*. On Sunday evenings Mr. Haskell rapped on our door and without a word, like a lord, handed us the "jokes" and the delectable magazine with its tales of high society, curly pictures, and horrifying medical stories illustrated in toothsome detail.

Mrs. Haskell avoided the Herman children. Tobie was beyond her understanding; her gentle, cowlike decorum knew no defense against such ferocity. She found us easier, especially myself; my brother moved too fast and erratically. She was, I now realize, lonely, and being shy of the bustling women around her, welcomed the snooping of a curious little girl. One Indian summer day when the four doors of the landing were open for cooler air, she invited me into her neat apartment, the furniture still and stolid, the curtains in stiff, regular folds, standing like school monitors. She told me to sit down and gave me a Lorna Doone and a Fig Newton, asking politely how school was and was my father going on strike. She had read about it in the papers and hoped it wouldn't happen. And did I know the world was going to end on October 20? Mr. Anderson, the leader of her Pure Christian Believers meetings, had said so and that God would take only his special people with him while he destroyed the rest. I believed her; I believed everything that was strange, preferably cataclysmic. Was Mr. Haskell going, too? No, he wasn't a Believer and so God couldn't, of course, include him among the Protected. I wanted yearningly to be taken, not to have to suffer a terrible holocaust like the people trying to flee the blood-red eruptions of Vesuvius that hung in our hallway. I doubted, though, that her Christian God with his blond hair and soft blond beard would take a Jewish child. We had to depend on the dour old man with the blazing eyes and windy white beard, like Moses who was inclined to favor few, if any.

Mrs. Haskell also told me that she was beginning to prepare for the Coming. Everything in her house, every salt shaker and frying pan was to be scrubbed, the sheets and towels boiled, every fork and knife polished—rather like Yom Kippur preparations. And then she was going to get herself ready, a bath every day for two weeks, her hair washed every other day, her toenails cut, the wax taken out of her ears, all of her clean and pure.

For several days I looked for her when I returned from school but she, almost always housebound, was away. I waited and watched, running out one evening as I heard her unlock her door.

She was carrying fancy boxes like the kind Barbara La Marr opened when a rich, infatuated admirer sent her a present. The boxes bore the noble letters, MACY'S, a legendary world where no one else I knew had ever wandered. She invited me to come in and, still in her hat and coat, opened the large box from which she lifted, very daintily, a long white nightgown with long sleeves and a high neck. It was beautiful. I wanted one like it and to live among blond angels who sang all day and not to die as part of a mountainous garbage heap. Still, I couldn't ask her to take me along, worried and quiet as she showed me her new pair of white laced oxfords like those the school nurse wore. A few days later she arrived with two smaller Macy boxes, one with a white nurse's cap in it and another that held the whitest cotton gloves. I asked her if she would go to bed to wait, in her new shoes and cap and gloves, seeing her laid out like a corpse. She said no, she was going into Eternal Life, not ordinary death, and would sit on her sofa covered with its new white sheet.

The anxious days went by, very slow and too fast. I could hardly speak to Mrs. Haskell, who had become as awesome as the Statue of Liberty. My mother was annoyed with me, inattentive, restless, brooding, darting toward the hallway whenever I thought I heard the Haskell door opening. Once my mother asked me, "What's the matter with you?" The answer was, "Nothing." We learned early to keep worries about God and sex to ourselves.

The tremendous day came. I awoke very early and slipped quietly out of our apartment and down into the street to observe warnings: people falling about, dogs trembling, cats dead, the sky glowering menace. The sky was blue, the clouds were tumbling like clowns, two sparrows picked at the manure left by the old-clothes-man's horse, Grandpa Paladino in his droopy pants and Old Country undershirt was frowning at his tomato plant. In school that day I kept watching the sky, waiting for it to crack

open like an immense ripe plum and pour fire and black smoke. I
ran home from school at lunchtime, the October wind snapping
at my bare knees. Mrs. Haskell's door was closed but I saw her
clearly in her white clothing on her white sofa, docile and patient
as always. Lunch was my favorite, broad noodles with pot cheese
and white raisins, sugar and cinnamon sprinkled on top, and the
pleasure it gave brought solace and relief as well. Maybe this End
of the World, like Christmas and Easter Sunday, was for Christians only, the good ones flying gently up to Heaven, guided by
God's hand, and the bad stabbed by lightning and dropped into
the ocean. The Jews would go on doing their homework, cooking, scolding, working in factories.

What about Mrs. Polanski, our janitor? What about the black
Gypsies who wandered through the streets, begging like cursing?
Would Miss Monahan, my favorite teacher, be in school the next
day? Mr. Jameson the principal, Mr. Keenan who opened the
school doors? Where would all the *goyim* of my life be? I would
miss the picture in Christian kitchens of the fat-legged baby who
sat in the lap of the pale lady with the golden ring around her
head. Who would keep a little goat tied to a stake in a backyard?
Would I ever be able to touch, very lightly (it might be a sin), a
real Christmas tree? Who would talk like singing, as Patrick the
milkman did? Would I never again see the thin blue eyelids, fine
as butterfly wings, of Jimmy and Mary O'Neill? The world
would be as full of holes as an old blanket but, nevertheless, I
would stay triumphantly alive.

The night of the 20th disappeared and so did the following
days and nights. I saw Mr. Haskell go to work and return, but no
Mrs. Haskell. All the Christians were in school and the Italians sat
on their porches, but I wasn't worried much about them because
they were just Jews who didn't talk Yiddish. They didn't go to
synagogues, either, but a lot of Jews didn't. Most of them went to
church only on their high holy days, like Jews. They bothered

their kids, kissed them and shouted at them, like Jews. Their old people, mumbling in old languages, also sat in the big chairs and were listened to. The clinching proof of this conviction was a rumor—I could hardly believe it—that the fat-legged baby who grew up to be a sad man wearing a circle of thorns was a Jew. Killed by other Jews. (That I couldn't believe at all; Jews didn't kill, they were killed in pogroms.)

Much happened during the next few days. My brother broke two front teeth, somehow my fault. The nurse with the terrible boiling face found nits in my hair and I walked home from school wrapped in flames of anger and humiliation. I hated the nurse, I hated my mother, I hated my brother who danced around me singing, "She's got nits. My dirty sister's got nits." When we reached the outer stairs of our apartment house, I ran ahead and turned to kick him full in the face, intending to kill him, or at least break his taunting mouth. There were, of course, consequences, and for days I seethed, forgetting Mrs. Haskell, until her door opened one afternoon as I arrived from school. With her usual courtesy, she asked me to visit with her for a few minutes. She offered me a Tootsie Roll and a new penny from the pocket of her pink flowered housedress and then turned to polishing her furniture, slowly, carefully. While she polished, she told me that God had come on October 20th. Not really, actually, come into her house but she had seen his long, pale hand in the sky pointing toward her and heard his gentle voice say, "Patience," "Soon," "Keep ready." Mr. Anderson had said the same thing at last night's meeting and would let them know when to start their purifications again, when to put on their white robes. Would she let me know the next time? No—she gave me a Fig Newton—this time it would have to be a secret for the Pure only.

Whenever we met, we avoided each other's eyes, although Mr. Haskell nodded politely. Then came a roaring Sicilian wedding, came the funeral of a grandfather who had a gnawing crab in his belly, came Rudolph Valentino in *The Sheik*, came the first bitter winds and conflicts over wearing lumpy, itchy, shaming winter underwear, came the flu whose fever made beautiful pictures swim in my head. Fannie Herman found pink worms in little David's anus and almost tore our door down in her panic. Esther Goldstein, sixteen and incandescent, so luminous that I could hardly look at her, said I was "odd" and killed me. Time erased and destroyed its events to make room for others, while Barney Google, the Captain and the Kids, and Mutt and Jeff kept coming every Sunday evening from the Haskells'. No news, ever again, of a Visitation.

Immediately to the left of us lived the Silverbergs. Manya Silverberg was dashing and pretty, younger than my mother and more stylish, with an impressive repertory of clothing that she made herself. She cooked well and made cookies that were more "American" than my mother's little pockets of hard tack known as cheese cookies. Like my mother, she was soft-spoken, a reader and a learner; both moved like debased aristocrats through the slatternly street of dented garbage cans on their way to English classes at the local public library. I loved Mrs. Silverberg as I loved Lillian Gish, as I loved the pretty young aunts, still in Warsaw, in the photographs I stared at for long times, trying to invent voices for them, improvising dialogues with them. She became a substitute aunt. And then she disappeared, after a midnight explosion. Since the bed my brother and I shared was nearest the door, we reached it first when we heard loud voices in the hallway. We were quickly shooed back to bed, our bedroom door closed on us firmly. But I had already seen the high color, the brown burning eyes. the waterfalls of earrings, brooches, and layers of pearls heaped like a five-and-ten counter on the ordinarily chaste neck. On the disordered dark hair a wide, swooping, arrogant hat and a big shawl draped around her shoulders like a movie star's evening cloak. High, loud, without a pause, in a torrential rain of words she spoke of going out to a fancy restaurant, of men, many men, waiting for her, of meeting with her lover, Rudolph Valentino, of dancing to cabaret music. She shrieked happiness hideously.

It was difficult after that to be absolutely certain of what was sane or insane, one world slid in and out of the other with confusing ease, particularly confusing when the word "*me-shugge*," crazy, was used so profligately for stamping and hollering with a Victrola record, for begging for new skates, for destroyed Mrs. Silverberg.

The lower landings were more remote, shaping their own looser tribes. A number of our friends lived in various sections of the house and we knew some of their parents, of little consequence to us unless they were unusually hospitable or unusually forbidding. The only fourth-floor family that steadily interested me were the Liebowitzes. Ida Liebowitz, who was in my class, wore long stockings and long sleeves winter and summer, a cruel piece of religious fanaticism according to the other mothers. She had no skates, wasn't permitted to go to the movies, ever, and on Saturdays read her library books on her fire escape away from the eyes of her father, Yontiff ("Holiday"), who would not permit the handling of *goyish* books on the Sabbath. He once caught her at it and tore the book out of her hands, thrusting it far onto the empty lot. There were fierce, unspecified punishments for losing library books, a sin as terrible as stealing or playing doctor. Ida might be sent to prison or left back in school or made to stay in every afternoon writing a hundred times "I must not lose library books." We all worried. Ida was not permitted to leave her house, the free-roaming boys would not stoop to search for a girl's book, and the girls, eager for the drama of the search, were told to "stay home and mind your own business." In any case, we hadn't much time. Last night's gefilte fish wrapped in its quivering coat of jelly and the chunks of *challa* were already on the table to be gobbled fast so we could get to the Belmont movie theater when it opened.

We almost immediately lost interest in the book and in the Liebowitzes, who soon moved to what the women called a more "kosher" neighborhood, with more piety, fewer *goyim*, and fewer of the even more dangerous Jewish *goyim* who let their children skate on Saturday and go to libraries and movies on Saturday, handling money to view the abominations of Sodom and Gomorrah. All we ever knew of Mrs. Liebowitz was that she wore a dull brown wig and never joined the conclaves of women and baby carriages on the street; she was as cloistered as a nun. He was bearded and frowning, like a picture-book pirate, except that he wore a dark hat. The Liebowitzes' door was always tight shut, even in the heat of August, and we kids who were free with several houses, running in and out except of course when floors were being washed or a new baby had been born, never saw the inside of their apartment. Nor did we play much with the Liebowitz children, who were not allowed in the corrupting street except to go directly to school and come directly home. Although I hardly knew them, I liked them or rather the idea of them, their secret lives, their fierce separateness, a cave people, a woods people like those who glowered out of fairy-tale darknesses. I missed them after they moved, very briefly.

5

The Movies and Other Schools

Life on Lafontaine offered several schools. School-school, P.S. 59, was sometimes nice, as when I was chosen to be Prosperity in the class play, blond, plump, dressed in a white pillow case banded with yellow and green crepe paper, for the colors of grasses and grain, and waving something like a sheaf of wheat. The cringing days were usually Fridays, when arithmetic flash cards, too fast, too many, blinded me and I couldn't add or subtract the simplest numbers. (For many years, into adulthood, I carried around a sack of churning entrails on Friday mornings.) The library, which made me my own absolutely special and private person with a card that belonged to no one but me, offered hundreds of books, all mine and no tests on them, a brighter, more generous school than P.S. 59. The brightest, most informative school was the movies. We learned how tennis was played and golf, what a swimming pool was and what to wear if you ever got to drive a car. We learned how tables were set, "How do you do? Pleased to meet you," how primped and starched little girls should be, how neat and straight boys should be, even when they were temporarily ragamuffins. We learned to look up soulfully and make our lips tremble to warn our mothers of a flood of tears, and though they didn't fall for it (they laughed), we kept practicing. We learned how regal mothers were and how stately fathers, and of course we learned about Love, a very foreign country like maybe China or Connecticut. It was smooth and slinky, it shone and rustled. It was petals with Lillian Gish, gay flags with Marion Davies, tiger stripes with Rudolph Valentino, dog's eyes with Charlie Ray. From what I could see, and I searched, there was no Love on the block, nor even its fairy-tale end, Marriage. We had only Being Married, and that included the kids, a big crowded barrel with a family name stamped on it. Of course, there was Being Married in the movies, but except for the terrible cruel people in rags and scowls, it was as silky as Love. Fathers kissed their wives and children when they came home from work and spoke to them quietly and nobly, like kings, and never shouted or hit if the kids came in late or dirty. Mothers in crisp dresses stroked their children's heads tenderly as they presented them with the big ringletted doll and the football Grandma had sent, adding, "Run off and play, darlings." "Darling," "dear," were movie words, and we had few grandmothers, most of them dead or in shadowy conversation pieces reported from At Home, the Old Country. And "Run off and play" was so superbly refined, silken gauze to the rough wool of our hard-working mothers whose rules were to feed their children, see that they were warmly dressed in the wintertime, and run to the druggist on Third Avenue for advice when they were sick. Beyond that it was mostly "Get out of my way." Not all the mothers were so impatient. Miltie's mother helped him with his arithmetic home-work; my mother often found us amusing and laughed with and at us a lot. From other apartments, on rainy afternoons: Joey— "What'll I do, Maaa?" His Mother—"*Va te ne! Gherradi!*" (the Italian version of "Get out of here"); Lily—"What'll I do, Maaa?"

Mrs. Stavicz—"Scratch your ass on a broken bottle." I sometimes wished my mother would say colorful, tough things like that but I wasn't sure I wouldn't break into tears if she did, which would make her call me a *"pianovi chasto"* (as I remember the Polish phrase), a delicate meringue cake that falls apart easily, which would make me cry more, which would make her more lightly contemptuous, and so on. Despite my occasional wish to see her as one of the big-mouth, storming women, I was willing to settle for her more modest distinction, a lady who won notebooks in her English class at the library and sang many tunes from "Polish operettas" that, with later enlightenment, I realized were *The Student Prince* and *The Merry Widow.*

Being Married had as an important ingredient a nervous father. There must have been other kitchens, not only ours, in which at about seven o'clock, the fathers' coming-home time, children were warned, "Now remember, Papa is coming home soon. He's nervous from working in the factory all day and riding in the crowded El. Sit quiet at the table, don't laugh, don't talk." It was hard not to giggle at the table, when my brother and I, who played with keen concentration a game of mortal enemies at other times, became close conspirators at annoying Them by making faces at each other. The muffled giggles were stopped by a shout of "Respect!" and a long black look, fork poised like a sword in midair while no one breathed. After the silent meal, came the part we disliked most, the after-dinner lecture. There were two. The first was The Hard Life of the Jewish worker, the Jewish father, the deepest funereal sounds unstopped for the cost of electricity (a new and lovely toy but not as pretty as throbbing little mazda lamps) for which he had to pay an immense sum each time we switched it on and off, like the wastrels we were. Did we think butter cost a penny a pound that we slathered it on bread as if it were Coney Island mud pies? Those good expensive shoes he bought us (he was an expert shoe worker, a maker of samples, and tortured us with embarrassment when he displayed his expertise to the salesman, so don't try to fool him), which were old and scuffed and dirty within a week, did we know how much bloody sweat was paid for them? The second lecture was the clever one whose proud, sententious repetitions I listened to with shame for him, wanting to put my head down not to see my handsome father turn into a vaudeville comic whose old monologues strained and fell. This lecture was usually inspired by my brother who, in spite of the "nervous" call, dashed at my father as soon as he heard the key in the lock with "Hello, Pa. Gimme a penny?" That led it off: "You say you want a penny, *only* a penny. I've got dimes and quarters and half-dollars in my pockets, you say, so what's a penny to me? Well, let's see. If you went to the El station and gave the man four cents, he wouldn't let you on the train, you'd need another penny. If Mama gave you two cents for a three-cent ice cream cone, would Mrs. Katz in the candy store give it to you? If Mama had only forty-eight cents for a forty-nine-cent chicken, would the butcher give it to her?" And on and on, a carefully rehearsed long slow aria, with dramatic runs of words and significant questioning pauses. Once or twice I heard my mother mutter as she went out of the room, "That Victrola record again," but her usual policy was to say nothing. She was not afraid of my father, nor particularly in awe of him. (I heard him say frequently how fresh she was, but with a smile, not the way he said it to us.)

In none of my assiduous eavesdropping on the street did I ever hear any mention of unhappy marriage or happy marriage. Married was married. Although a Jewish divorce was a singularly easy matter except for the disgrace it carried, the Jewish women were as firmly imbedded in their marriages as the Catholic. A divorce was as unthinkable as adultery or lipstick. No matter what—beatings, infidelity, drunkenness, verbal abuse, outlandish demands—no woman could run the risk of making her children fatherless. Marriage and children were fate, like being skinny, like skeletal Mr. Roberts, or humpbacked, like the leering watchman at the hat factory. "*Es is mir beschert*," "It is my fate," was a common sighing phrase, the Amen that closed hymns of woe.

My mother didn't accept her fate as a forever thing. She began to work during our school hours after her English classes had taught her as much as they could, and while I was still young, certainly no more than ten, I began to get her lecture on being a woman. It ended with extraordinary statements, shocking in view of the street mores. "Study. Learn. Go to college. Be a schoolteacher," then a respected, privileged breed, "and don't get married until you have a profession. With a profession you can have men friends and even children, if you want. You're free. But don't get married, at least not until you can support yourself and make a careful choice. Or don't get married at all, better still." This never got into "My mother said" conversations with my friends. I sensed it to be too outrageous. My mother was already tagged "The Princess" because she never went into the street unless fully, carefully dressed: no grease-stained housedress, no bent, melted felt slippers. Rarely, except when she was pregnant with my little sister, did she stop for conversations on the street. She was one of the few in the building who had gone to classes, the only mother who went out alone at night to join her mandolin group. She was sufficiently marked, and though I was proud of her difference, I didn't want to report her as altogether eccentric. In the community fabric, as heavy as the soups we ate and the dark, coarse "soldier's bread" we chomped on, as thick as the cotton on which we practiced our cross-stitch embroidery, was the conviction that girls were to marry as early as possible, the earlier the more triumphant. (Long after we moved from the area, my mother, on a visit to Lafontaine to see appealing, inept little Fannie Herman who had for many years been her charge and mine, met Mrs. Roth, who asked about me. When my mother said I was going to Hunter College, Mrs. Roth, looking both pleased and sympathetic, said, "*My* Helen married a man who makes a nice living, a laundry man. Don't worry, your Katie will find a husband soon." She knew that some of the boys of the block wound up in City College, but a girl in college? From a pretty, polite child, I must have turned into an ugly, bad-tempered shrew whom no one would have. Why else would my marrying years be spent in college?)

I never saw my mother and father kiss or stroke each other as people did in the movies. In company she addressed him, as did most of the Jewish women, by our family name, a mark of respectful distance. They inhabited two separate worlds, he adventuring among anti-Semites to reach a shadowy dungeon called "Factory," where he labored ceaselessly. In the evening he returned to her world for food, bed, children, and fighting. We were accustomed to fighting: the boys and, once in a while, fiery little girls tearing at each other in the street; bigger Italian boys punching and being punched by the Irish gangs that wandered in from Arthur Avenue; females fighting over clotheslines—whose sheets were blocking whose right to the sun—bounced around the courtyard constantly. The Genoese in the houses near 178th Street never spoke to the Sicilians near 179th Street except to complain that somebody's barbaric little southern slob had peed against a northern tree. To my entranced ears and eyes, the Sicilians seemed always to win, hotter, louder, faster with "*Fangu*"—the southern version of "*Fa' in culo*" (up yours)—than the aristocrats who retired before the Sicilians could hit them with "*Mortacci*"—the utterly insupportable insult. My brother and I fought over who grabbed the biggest apple, who hid the skate key, and where he put my baby picture, I lying on a white rug with my bare ass showing, a picture he threatened to pass among his friends and humiliate me beyond recovery. I would have to kill him.

These sorts of fighting were almost literally the spice of daily life, deliciously, lightly menacing, grotesque and entertaining. The fighting between my mother and father was something else entirely, at times so threatening that I still, decades later, cringe in paralyzed stupidity, as if I were being pelted with stones, when I hear a man shouting. The fights often concerned our conduct and my mother's permissiveness. My father had a rich vocabulary which he shaped into theatrical phrases spoken in a voice as black and dangerous as an open sewer. The opening shot was against my brother, who was six or seven when the attacks began. He was becoming a wilderness boy, no sense, no controls, dirty, disobedient, he did badly in school (not true: with a minimum of attention he managed mediocrity). There was no doubt that he would become a bum, then a thief, wind up alone in a prison cell full of rats, given one piece of bread a day and one cup of dirty water. He would come out a gangster and wind up in the electric chair.

When it was my turn, I was disobedient and careless; I didn't do my homework when I should, I didn't practice enough, my head was always in a book, I was always in the street running wild with the Italian and Polish beasts. I didn't take proper care of my brother, I climbed with boys, I ran with boys, I skated with them on far streets. Mr. Kaplan had seen me and told him. And how would this life, this playing with boys, end? I would surely become a street girl, a prostitute, and wind up being shipped to a filthy, diseased brothel crawling with hairy tropical bugs, in Buenos Aires. My mother's response was sharp and short: we acted like other children and played like other children; it was he who was at fault, asking more of us than he should. And enough about prisons and electric chairs and brothels. He went on shouting, entranced by his gorgeous words and visions, until she left the room to wash the dishes or scrub the kitchen floor. We, of course, had heard everything from our bedroom; the oratory was as much for us as for our mother. When the big rats in the windowless cell came to our ears, my brother began to shake with terror beyond crying. I tried to comfort him, as accustomed a role as trying to maim him. I didn't know what a street girl was, and I certainly didn't know what a brothel was, but I wasn't afraid—I was too angry. If our father hated us so, why didn't he go away? I didn't examine consequences, who would feed us and pay the rent. I just wanted him out, out, dead.

Other fights were about money, and that, too, involved us. How dare she, without consulting him, change from a fifty-cent-a-lesson piano teacher to another—and who knows how good *he* was?—who charged a dollar? What about the embroidered tablecloth and the stone bowl with the pigeons that she bought from the Arab peddler, that crook. Did she realize how hard he had to work to pay for our school supplies each fall? And add to that the nickel for candy to eat at the movies every Saturday, and the ten cents each for the movie and the three cents for ice-cream cones on Friday nights. And God only knew how much money she slipped us for the sweet garbage we chewed on, which would certainly rot our teeth, and where would he get the money for dentists? Maybe she thought she was still in her shop in Warsaw, dancing and singing and spilling money like a fool. And on and on it went. These tirades, too, were answered very briefly. Our lives were meager enough. Did he ever think of buying us even the cheapest toy, like the other fathers did, instead of stashing every spare penny in the bank and taking it out only for his relatives? The ignorant Italians he so despised, they had celebrations for their children. Where were our birthday presents?

Long silences followed these fights and we became messengers. "Tell your mother to take my shoes to the shoemaker." "Aw, Pa, I'm doing my homework. Later." "Tell your mother I have no clean shirts." "Aw, Pa, I'm just sitting down to practice. I'll tell her later." We used the operative words "homework" and "practice" mercilessly while he seethed at our delays. My mother heard all these instructions but it was her role neither to notice nor to obey. Those were great days and we exploited our roles fattily, with enormous vengeful pleasure.

One constant set of squabbles that didn't circle around us concerned her relaxed, almost loose judgments of other people. She showed no sympathy when he complained about the nigger sweeper in the factory who talked back to him, when he complained about the Italian who reeked of garlic and almost suffocated him in the train. Most loudly he complained about her availability, spoiling his sleep, letting his supper get cold, neglecting her own children, to run to any Italian idiot who didn't know to take care of her own baby. Let them take care of their own convulsions or get some Wop neighbor to help. It was disgraceful that she sat on Mrs. Santini's porch in open daylight trying to teach her not to feed her infant from her own mouth. If the fat fool wanted to give it germs, let her. If it died, she'd, next year, have another; they bred like rabbits. Why didn't my mother mind her own business, what the hell did these people, these foreign ignoramuses, mean to her? The answer was short and always the same, "*Es is doch a mench,*" yet these are human beings, the only religious training we ever had, perhaps quite enough.

There were fights with no messengers, no messages, whispered fights when the door to our bedroom was shut tight and we heard nothing but hissing. The slow unfolding of time and sophistications indicated that these were fights about women, women my father saw some of those evenings when he said he was going to a Workmen's Circle meeting. There was no more "Tell your mother," "Tell your father," and except for the crying of our baby, no more evening sounds. No Caruso, no Rosa Ponselle, no mandolin practice, no lectures. My father busied himself with extra piecework, "skiving" it was called, cutting with breathtaking delicacy leaf and daisy designs into the surface of the sample shoes to be shown to buyers. She, during one such period, crocheted a beaded bag, tiny beads, tiny stitches. We watched, struck dumb by their skill, and because it was no time to open our mouths about anything, anything at all. The silence was dreadful, a creeping, dark thing, a night alley before the murderer appears. The furniture was waiting to be destroyed, the windows to be broken, by a terrible storm. We would all be swept away, my brother and I to a jungle where wild animals would eat us, my parents and the baby, separated, to starve and burn alone in a desert. School now offered the comforts of a church, the street its comforting familiarities, unchanging, predictable. We stayed out as long as we could, dashing up for a speedy supper, and down again. On rainy nights we read a lot, we went to bed early, anything to remove us from our private-faced parents, who made us feel unbearably shy.

One spring evening, invited to jump Double Dutch with a few experts, uncertain that I could leap between two ropes whipping in rapid alternation at precisely the exact moment, and continue to stay between them in small fast hops from side to side, I admitted a need, urgent for some time, to go to the toilet. I ran up the stairs to find our door locked, an extraordinary thing. Maybe they had run away. Maybe they had killed each other. Sick with panic, I kept trying the door, it wouldn't give. Then I heard the baby making squirmy, sucking baby noises. No matter what, my mother would never leave the baby, and anyway, maybe they were doing their whispering fighting again. Still uneasy, I knocked on the Hermans' door and asked to use their toilet. When I came out, I asked Fannie Herman if she knew whether my parents were at home. Yes, she said. Her door was wide open and she would have seen or heard them come out, but they hadn't. The Double Dutch on the street was finished when I got down so I joined the race, boys and girls, around the block, running hard, loving my pumping legs and my swinging arms and my open mouth swallowing the breeze. When most of the kids had gone home and it was time for us, too, I couldn't find my brother, who was hiding from me to destroy my power and maybe get me into trouble. I went up alone. The door had been unlocked, and as I walked uneasily through the long hallway of our railroad flat with wary steps, I heard sounds from the kitchen. My mother was sitting on a kitchen chair, her feet in a basin of water. My father was kneeling before her on spread newspaper. Her plump foot rested in his big hand while he cut her toenails, flashing his sharp work knife, dexterous, light, and swift. She was splashing him a little, playing the water with her free foot. They were making jokes, lilting, laughing. Something, another branch in the twisted tree that shaded our lives, was going to keep us safe for a while.

6

Summer Fruits

One of the summer pleasures was to sit at the kitchen window and listen to the polyphony of courtyard noises out of twenty other kitchens. Early in the morning came the screech of clotheslines being pulled to and from the big pole at the back of the yard that supported the lines of both 2029 and 2027, an admirable grandfather pole sustaining so many children. At that time there wasn't much talk across the yard; there was too much to do, like getting the kids' breakfast, a nice collection of noises: "Finish your breakfast, you can't go out before you do"; "*Schloch* [slob]! Look what you did to the dress I just ironed"; "Tie your laces so you don't fall"; in several weary tones, "Don't bother me. Get dressed first and then you'll talk"; "No, you can't go to Mannie's house, his sister has chicken pox"; "Here's a nickel for a new ball; if you lose this one, you won't get another." The heavier sounds of exasperation came later with the heavier heat of the day: a crash, a slap, and "I'll break your hands if you touch that china closet again," and as leitmotif, a broken chorus of "*Geddade,*" also pronounced "*Gerrare*" and "*Gherradi,*" depending on the national origin of the shouter. The litany of Jewish curses, calls, and wisecracks that became bright spots in immigrant literature were lacking in our courtyard. We never heard the famous bread call: "Ma, cut me off and butter me up and throw me down a piece of bread." Ours was the less colorful, less musical, "Ma, I want a piece of bread." (Not from 5B in 2029, though; this was too much country manners for my parents and strictly forbidden.) Of the numerous references to trolley cars quoted in the literature, we never heard the gorgeously picturesque "May a trolley car grow in your belly that you may piss nickels and shit transfers [or vice versa]." My father would answer my mother's conjectures when he was in a playful mood with "If, if. If my grandmother had wheels, she'd be a trolley car," and better yet, "If my grandmother had a penis, she'd be my grandfather." The most stimulating local curse came from Ruthie Rosen's kitchen, on the third floor of 2027: "May you grow like an onion with your head in the ground and your feet in the air." During my early encounters with this image, I examined Rosie to see if her head was bending to the ground and her feet flying off the sidewalk, as her mother said they must be. She stayed the same mouse-faced little girl, skinny and erect as a ruler—another ground for skepticism.

The afternoon sounds were "Practice. Go practice. Now, I say," and the assembled pianos cranked out the wobbling sounds of an immense broken merry-go-round. From three pianos the thumping, sure or tentative, of "Für Elise" competing with tortured gropings from everyone's primer, "Bayer's Book." From the first floor of 2029, a merry reckless bumbling through Tchaikovsky's "Troika" colliding with a comet of scales from the first floor of 2027. When it all faded out, the crickets on the long Monterey lots covered the afternoon with their rustling taffeta sound. The "Ole Close" men called as the sun began to pale, never doing a brisk trade. Old clothes were sent to relatives in the Old Country. The yard singers did better with their mixed repertoire of "O Sole Mio," "Eli Eli," "Delia, Oh Delia," and "Daisy, Daisy." It wasn't only the singing and the romantic presence of a street singer but the luxury of giving away money for something intangible that spurred us kids to hop around our mothers nagging for two pennies, three. We wrapped them securely in large wads of newspaper and flung them down, feeling like lords. The hour of clanging pots and "Wash yourself, you look like the coalman," was the hour of the opening and closing doors and "Hello, Pop," followed by threnodies of complaint. They were short bursts, stifled by a large, round "Shut up. Let me sit and have my supper first." During the quiet of supper, the birds who had been hiding from the kids on the lot all day began to call and sing a little, timidly, as if they were still scared of boys with sticks. The later hours were parents' time, a rich tapestry—if one could stay awake long enough—of Victrola horns spilling jigs and reels, Alma Gluck, Yosele Rosenblatt, Caruso, "When You and I Were Young, Maggie," Sousa marches, flowing through and over and around the banging of chairs and doors, the weeping and shouting of adult quarrels, never quite clear enough for the clouds of music around them. Very late and the yard's final "Good night," the small gasps and whistles of snoring from open bedroom windows.

The shapes of things changed in the summertime. The smoke from the hat factory next door became fat and slow, oozing like a chorus of fat ladies in pink, blue, yellow, purple dresses. The edges of buildings shook and melted. Cold, dry faces opened and glistened with sweat. The spikey park flowers bent and hung. The sidewalks sweated, the walls sweated, and out of the heat and wetness came heavily ornate, lazy bunches of grapes, the opulent shine and swell of plums, the rubies of pomegranate seeds set in their yellow embroidery. (When I came to know Keats' "Ode to Autumn" and the Ingres women in his "Turkish Bath," they became again the languid airs and shapes of my childhood summers.)

Summertime was life, wide and generous, fat King Cole lolling on his throne listening to his fiddlers three, a smiling dolphin turning, playing in big, shining waters. Summer was another country whose fathers had, suddenly, bare, shy arms, whose mothers padded like cats on bare feet. Time was still summer air, as slow and round as pregnant women. In the mornings, time sat quietly, waiting for me as I commanded it to, watching me think, shape, arrange the world. The breakfast farina and milk should be mountains and rivers and I heaped mounds and scraped tunnels with my spoon to make it so. The sun that lit up the rung of a chair, if it hid behind the cloud, would the chair become something else? And if I decided to call the chair a table and said it many times, would the back disappear and the seat broaden to become a table? My brother's pinches (he was still asleep; I hated sleeping, it stole things from me) hurt me. Why didn't I feel anything when I pinched him, just as hard? (I still find myself searching for that answer.)

Cloaked in the royal robes of omnipotent childhood, I went down—it was very early—to check the condition of my domain and my subjects. I was the queen of my block. No one but I knew it and I knew it well, each morning making a royal progress on my empty street, among my big garbage cans, my limp window curtains, my sheet of newspaper slowly turning and sliding in the gutter, my morning glory on Mrs. Roberti's porch vine, my waiting stoops fronting my sleeping houses; my hat factory on the corner of 179th Street, resting from its hours of blowing pink and blue and purple dye smoke; my Kleins, my Rizzos, my Petrides, my Clancys safely in bed, guarded by my strength and will. Even after I had been heavily assaulted with school proofs that very little of the world was mine, that history existed of itself and not as a huge crowded stage hurriedly arranged the day I was born, I maintained a deep interest in my subjects, moving out of absolute control to the more subtle control of observer and critic. (My father, no fool, sensing the menace inherent in the long stares half hidden by my thatch of flaxen hair, accused my mother of having brought forth a silent white snake.)

Early one July morning, the sidewalk already soft and steamy like the bed I had left, I made my usual surveillance, this morning the good fairy tiptoeing through the sleeping castle in the sleeping forest. All was well: the De Santis garage door was locked; the factory door was locked. The Morettis' gray cat was stalking a sparrow, and I hoped she would get it since she wasn't a good mouser and must have a disappointing life. As I watched the cat— a dummy, not good at sparrows either—the clanking of bars and the rumble of turning bolts told me that the factory doors were opening. The oldest De Santis boy, still chewing on a breakfast roll, came out of his stucco house to set a chair on the porch for his grandmother. Annie's father in his working cap, carrying a brown paper lunch bag, ran down the stairs of their house and turned briskly in the direction of the El station. Windows and doors shot open, the trickle of voices thickened, and the legs of the fathers on their way to work became a jumble of zigzags on the sidewalk. I watched my show, contented with its expectedness, hoping a little for the unexpected. Maybe Mr. Kaplan would be wearing his new hat to work, like the gentleman and hero he was. Two Sundays ago he had shouted up at a towering *goy* who wouldn't let him sit on a nearby park bench, "Because I'm a Jew and you're a Christian, I should kiss your ass? You can kiss *my* ass." If not Mr. Kaplan's hat, maybe Mrs. Santini would come out on her porch, chewing yesterday's spaghetti and pushing it into the mouth of her new baby, like what birds did, and then nurse it from a pale flood of breast. Maybe, with luck, I might see one of the sleek men who looked like knives, nobody's fathers or immigrant uncles, run quickly out of the houses of "*nafkas*," a word whispered by the mothers as they rocked their baby carriages in the street, a word, like many, I didn't quite understand yet sensed fairly accurately.

The stage was filling nicely. The milkman was coming around the corner, little boys—not my dopey brother, thank God—were tumbling into the streets. Suddenly, from around the corner, at the back of the factory, the sounds of yelping, wailing, shrieking. I ran, to see something Lon Chaney might have invented as a mad doctor. Dogs, back to back stuck together, trying to pull away from each other, screaming as they pulled. They snapped their teeth at the air, their eyes rolled in anguish, their legs arched and pawed in a crazy dance, their rumps rubbed and twisted, but they couldn't separate. Two factory workers stopped for a moment, watched, exchanged a phrase and a smile, and walked on. I couldn't understand why two grown men couldn't, wouldn't, separate the dogs who must have sat in some glue that was tearing their skins and fur as they pulled.

I ran back to my house and leaped up the tenement stairs, past the open doors that drew relief from the cool stone landings. Past Mrs. Petrides' floor, past Mrs. Schwartz's, past Mrs. Szekely's and up to our own, where Mrs. Haskell, with no children to feed or dress, sat reading love advice, fanning herself with the rest of the *Graphic*. I gasped "Hello" and dashed into our apartment. "Mama! Mama! Come down quick. There are two dogs stuck together, maybe some mean person glued them. They can't separate and it hurts them. They're screaming. Please, Mama, it's terrible, get them apart."

The expected move to the door didn't happen. Even with her new big belly, my mother would run down the four flights when Marie Moretti shouted up from the stairwell that her mother's new baby was twisting funny, or when Mrs. Bernstein called across the yard that her stinking old father was sick and needed cupping. Now she stood at the stove and continued stirring the soup as she poured in barley. "Please, Ma, please hurry."

"No. I'm staying here and so are you. Mind your own business. Play in the house." The round face and the mouth like summer fruit had become dry and flat, she looked like the assistant principal, an iron lady. Another "Please" would have been useless, I knew. I must have done something wrong and I went away from the strange woman as far as I could, to the back fire escape to watch the colored smoke from the factory fade into the sky I counted the mattresses flopping out of the open windows on Monterey Avenue, across from the empty lot below. I took out my box of cloth scraps to try the pink with the blue; no, the yellow with the blue, the shiny with the dull; two shinys. I was going to stay on the fire escape forever, burn in the sun, freeze in the snow, never go back into the kitchen with the woman with the stone face and the ugly humpback on her belly. She called me in for a glass of milk. I went and drank it in the kitchen, both of us very quiet, a nervous quiet like the first day in a new class. I shouldn't have told her about the dogs. I didn't ask her why. She didn't tell me.

The day of the glued dogs led off many watchful days, days of going out only with Mama. I was her helper, her monitor, much, much older now than my brother, in gray shade while he darted and dazzled in the full sun of the street. They were slow troublesome walks. I didn't want to be with her when her belly burst open and spilled a hundred tiny babies like watermelon seeds. Or it might crack open and a skinny little blind chick would fall to the sidewalk, or out of the crack would slide the long, shining blue of a skinless rabbit like those on the hooks of the Italian butcher shop. I couldn't say I wouldn't go with her, but I hated this swollen person who used to be as lively as jumping rope and never scared. Now she was scared when she stepped off the sidewalk, scared of the boxes flung around in the market, scared of crippled people and Mary Sugar Bum, who staggered around singing like a penny whistle. Once her skirt caught in a band of metal on the stair rail. She tripped, lost her footing, but didn't fall, nothing to make a fuss about. But she sat down on one of the steps and burst into tears. I couldn't understand why, nothing had happened, she hadn't even torn her skirt or scraped her knee and I hadn't ever seen her cry except when she laughed very hard. She was becoming a big ugly crybaby, and lazy. She had to rest a lot and I didn't really know what "resting" meant. She told me to go down and play but I wouldn't. I sat in the kitchen reading about and envying the Dutch Twins who clomped around in noisy wooden shoes—and people let them—or ice-skated and ice-skated all day through the winter. Sometimes I would take, very careful with the latch, a few cherries from the icebox. I ate them slowly, stroking the silk skin, looking at the way the stems jumped up like dancers, crunching into the juicy blood red and sucking the pit until it, too, felt like silk. While I examined and bit and sucked, I heard from across the courtyard Ruthie rumbling her way through scales on her new piano and the sighs of steam from the factory.

Our walks grew shorter, the descent down the stairs slow and careful, I gripping her hand, bracing myself against the pull of the belly, maybe ready to fall and bounce like an enormous ball, thudding down, down, along the four flights of stairs and into the street. As the descent became more difficult—and frightening, I suppose—my mother stopped for a few minutes of what the men referred to as "women's talk" with the neighbors before we went on toward the park or around the block. While they talked, I bounced my ball, staying as close as I discreetly could to the low words. "They had to pull the baby from her with instruments. She screamed for two days." "She always lost them in the fourth month." "The cord got twisted around the neck, so it died."

Bounce, bounce, bounce, foot over the ball on the fourth bounce, waiting for the key words, how a baby got into a belly and just how it got out, but they never came. There was repeated mention of nine months. Did that mean that it took nine months for a baby to ripen like a banana to be peeled, a peach to be sliced when it was ready? It must hurt, otherwise the women wouldn't be whispering about screaming. As I bounced the ball, a heat of terror and guilt burned through me and turned to icy nausea in my stomach. I had done this to my mother, made her shout with pain for hours and hours, while doctors dug and ripped at her with "instruments," big pliers and saws that tore her flesh and skin. No wonder my mother could get so mad at me sometimes for reasons I didn't understand. Bouncing, still bouncing the ball, I wondered why she didn't fight this baby off? Or maybe she didn't know it was coming in, like nits in hairs, like worms in puppies and babies? I kept waiting for words that would unlock the door the women guarded, for the light that would make everything clear and nice, like the neat gardens and the clear people with clear smiles in books.

Instead, the women moved into the commonness of headaches and sore throats, a winding, boring exchange of symptoms and cures I'd heard before. But old Mrs. Rabinowitz was usually there and she said odd things. I bounced the ball and listened. Mrs. Rabinowitz was a kind of witch who, some of the women said, put curses on people. She had appeared one late Friday afternoon at the door of the Rosenbergs, asking for a match for her candles. Matches in hand, she looked in toward the dining room where the gleaming candlesticks and the shining *challa* rested on the table, sniffed the scrubbed smell of the house, the lemon oil on the furniture, the golden smell of chicken soup, watched the children rolling marbles down the apartment hall-way, stared at Mr. Rosenberg reading his paper in his comfortable chair. In her rough, deep voice as steady as her burning eyes she intoned, "I also had a husband. I also had children. Be careful. With God one makes no contracts." Mrs. Rosenberg pushed her out the door and ran from child to child, making three spitting sounds over the head of each to dispel the Evil Eye the old witch had brought in. Mrs. Rosenberg avoided her, would never talk to her after that. The other women were just as afraid of Mrs. Rabinowitz but preferred to keep on her good side because she was also a powerful healer; she might be useful someday. Who knows what God might send? So the women listened patiently as I did above the dull, light rhythm of the ball, as she told them what to do for the inflamed throats many of the children suffered each winter. "The mother must take her own stocking. It must be her own, it must be cotton, it must be black, no other color, only black. Then the mother must make water on it, and while it's still warm, wrap it around the child's throat. And she should do that each time she makes water until the child is better and that's in a day, always." My mother, a big-city girl and herself a reputable healer and not much concerned with the Evil Eye, asked, "But wouldn't warm water on a cloth do the same thing?" "No, never. How can water from a sink and a piece of old sheet be as good for a child as its mother's water and a stocking from her body? Foolish woman."

Fighting the stinking, wet stocking I imagined around my neck, fighting the horrors of birthing, I shouted in my head a powerful curse I had just read: "You're only a deck of cards!" They were all crazy, all those old people, peeing on black stockings, letting themselves have babies that hurt, whispering dumb secrets, and getting mad for nothing. I blew them away and ran to join a potsy game (books called it "hopscotch") chalked out on the sidewalk.

At the end of August that year, the temperature rose to near 100 and stayed, motionless, thick. It was too hot to walk, too hot to go to the library, too hot to play in the street. My brother took his train of spools down to Jimmy Petrides' house; Bianca's grandmother was sick so I couldn't swing in her yard, and I was mad at Becky, who stole my best pencil and denied it. I had finished reading the Belgian Twins and French Twins. I couldn't play with the big doll in the closet that had been there for two years. It was mine, bought for me by old Uncle David, but my father said I couldn't play with it, it was too good. (My brother broke it a year later, climbing up into the closet and down awkwardly, smashing her gorgeous, staring face to bits. He accused me of egging him on, and he was probably right, but I denied it, screaming anguish and hatred.) My mother suggested that if I was very careful, I might play with the bowls in the china closet and the basket of tiny flowers, but I must put them back very carefully. I didn't feel like being careful, so when she went to her room to lie down, I just sat and waited. I looked at the light behind the drawn window shade, listened to the crickets on the green lot, traced with my pinkie the red roses and green leaves stitched into the tablecloth in the dining room. When I heard my mother's light snoring, I slipped into the hall, through the open door and up the stairs to the roof.

This was my second kingdom, a continuous black, romantic terrain of tar and low brick dividers that marked off the houses, which stretched from one end of the block to the other. Here I could walk high above the street, in the sky and unshadowed sun. It was here that my subjects spent the hottest nights, when it became a place of dark figures dragging white sheets that billowed like sails and waves as they sank on spreads of newspaper. The sleepy children were put down to curl on each other, fitting like sections of orange. At one side of the pale patches of sheet, the fathers talked quietly while the mothers sat whispering on the other side. From the factory at the end of the row, dye vat vapors stained the thin, smoky dark of the summer night. On this slow-breathing afternoon there was no one around. The hot tar squeaked under my feet as I practiced stepping like Mae Murray with dainty, pointed toes over the brick dividers. I picked some of the hot shining tar from between the bricks and chewed it, a forbidden thing. It tasted of sun and dust, stiffer and better than bubble gum, better than rubber bands. As I chewed and pointed my toes, wondering how close I could get to the edge of the roof before I became too frightened, I heard funny little sounds. They seemed to come from behind a skylight of the middle houses. Like an Indian scout I moved carefully, watching out for the pebbles that might slide under my feet and, rattling, give me away. Following the little gasps and moans and giggles, I reached a side of the skylight from which I could peer around to the front. A man and woman were squirming together like big, tangled worms. Their clothing was all mixed up, open, closed; some off, some on. Clasping, turning, legs and arms grasping and lashing like an octopus, a behind thumping like an angry gorilla, they were stuck as the dogs were but not hurting. I watched for a while as their gasps and moans became shuddery little "Oohs" like being splashed with cold water. More crazies, getting dirty and sweaty, messing up their clothing, hugging, digging, twisting on the hot sticky tar.

I ran back to my skylight, forgetting the twinkle-toe steps, laughing and laughing. Down the stairs and into the apartment to tell my mother about this funny thing I saw. She was still on her bed, awake now and smiling. "What's so funny? What are you laughing at? What happened?" I was about to tell her when I looked at her face, the face that had turned to stone when I asked her to help the dogs. I looked at her belly; maybe the people on the roof were making a belly. Quite easily, smoothly, I began to play the secrets game, as comfortable in my evasions as grown-ups were. "Nothing much, Mama. Sarah was trying to imitate Nita Naldi. She was trying to slink vampy with her fat behind and pigeon toes." "Did she say anything? Tell me." "Nothing,

Ma, honest." "She probably said dirty words, that Sarah, didn't she?" "Yes, Mama." "Don't tell me then, don't repeat them." "All right, Mama, I won't."

All that day I could feel the laughter bubbling in me, I could see the whipping bodies of the dogs and the people mixed up with the swell of my mother's body. I washed my face and combed my hair without being told to; I cut the cucumbers neatly, in even slices, almost as well as my mother did, when I helped with supper. The tall door to their secret gardens was beginning, maybe just a crack, to open to me. I didn't know just what I knew, but I knew I was closer to knowing.

7

Birthing

He looked so much like a story character—the gentled Scrooge of a *St. Nicholas Magazine* Christmas issue, a not-too-skeletal Ichabod Crane—that it is difficult to say how he really looked. And he was ephemeral, his visits timed for the hours we were in school so that we caught only occasional glimpses of him as he strode around a corner, immensely tall (something we were not accustomed to in our Mediterranean street) and thin, wearing a long, skinny black coat and a shapeless black hat, carrying a black doctor's satchel. We knew Dr. James had visited when we found our mothers in bed "resting," an odd word, an odd event. When we left for school, they had no symptoms of cold or cough or pain; preoccupied perhaps, but that was common among women who worried about getting the rent paid on time, about shoes for the children, about husbands who habitually came home late from work. There was never an explanation for Dr. James's visit, what he did, what he said; only the mother on the bed, a peculiar worrisome thing, like finding the library or school suddenly, without warning, closed. By suppertime the mothers would be chopping, cutting, cooking, sometimes more quiet than usual, sometimes more irritable, nothing more.

When I became a member of a medical family that had practiced in the Bronx for decades, I once mentioned Dr. James and his unexplained short visits to mothers only, and never to deliver babies. A spate of enthusiastic information poured over the dinner table. Dr. James was, even when I knew him as a child, quite an old man, retired from a prestigious and lucrative practice in Boston, they thought. His was a prosperous intellectual family, the famous New England Jameses that produced William and Henry, but to the older Bronx doctors, *the* James was the magnificent old driven scarecrow. Having educated his children and seen their arrival into respected professions, he dedicated himself to poor immigrant women for whom there was no sex information, no birth-control clinics, nothing but knitting needles, hat pins, lengths of wire, the drinking of noxious mixtures while they sat in scalding baths to prevent the birth of yet another child. At times one woman would inflict these well-meant injuries on a sister, a neighbor; sometimes they were solitary acts of desperation. Some women died of septicemia; some of those who could not kill the fetus had to wait out the nine months and the delivery to let the infant die of exposure or suffocation.

To prevent such suicides and murders, Dr. James went from one immigrant neighborhood to another, performing abortions. (How he was informed where he was needed no one seemed to know; there must have been one woman in each area who transmitted messages.) He lived to be quite old and, according to my informants, worked vigorously at his self-appointed job until he died, having performed thousands of abortions, the fee a dollar or two or nothing, depending on the degree of poverty he met. Every adult in his neighborhoods knew him and his function, including cops and Board of Health people, who usually let him be. It was during the periodic sweeps of new brooms in office that he was arrested and imprisoned. He succumbed to it all very calmly, didn't call lawyers or his family, nor offered bail. Apparently he got in touch with one or two colleagues who called others, who in turn called others, and together they stormed the court where he was being tried. They pleaded, they argued, they shouted; they accused the police and the court of ignorance and inhumanity, and had him released. This drama was repeated several times, memorable times for the doctors who could thus demonstrate their admiration for the old man with the courage and independence to act as they might, if they but could.

Dr. James was a careful gynecologist as well as a skilled abortionist. There were women he would not abort. My little sister was much more gently handled, more eagerly cosseted, than my brother and I were because, my mother told me when we had become close adult friends, the baby was unwanted and was allowed to be born only because Dr. James refused to perform another abortion; she had had too many and another could be hazardous. How many she had I found out when I checked her into a hospital a few years before she died. Thirteen. I asked her again when we were alone in her hospital room whether I had heard correctly. Thirteen? And three children besides? Yes, and that was by no means the neighborhood record, she said. How could I account for the fact that a number of our Italian neighbors, urged by the Catholic Church to produce large families, had no more than two or three children? Certainly it wasn't the abstinence of Italian husbands, no more controlled than Jewish husbands. It was the work of the blessed hands of that wonderful old *goy*.

When school started in September before I was quite eight, the walks with my swollen mother—watching her skirt so that she didn't stumble on the stairs, pacing my steps, skipping in place to her lumbering, rocking walk, like the elephant in the zoo—

stopped. When we came home from school there was a quiet in the house that seemed to tremble against the walls, no lilting greetings, no apples and crackers on the table, in the sink a cold half cup of tea with milk. She was resting, and resting meant sick, like the times when Dr. James had come and gone. It also meant trouble. I kept glancing surreptitiously at her ankles to see if they were swollen. In scraps of eavesdropping I had accumulated something about women swelling and having convulsions before babies were born. My mother had swelled but didn't have convulsions when I was born, a difficult delivery, "with instruments" that dented my forehead. (Tracing the dent in my forehead, I wondered if it would squeeze my brains and someday make me crazy, like Mrs. Silverberg or my father's sister Surrele, whose name was thrown at me when I threw shoes and slammed doors.) "Instruments" were enormous black pincers, like those the iceman used to pull blocks of ice from his wagon, stuck in my mother's belly, ripping through the flesh and searching among her bleeding bowels until it hit my forehead and grabbed me, pulling up and out again through the red, messed flesh into the air, and dropped me, a doll covered with pee and shit, into hands that slapped to make me breathe. And now, in our house, a few paces from the kitchen, fewer from the dining room, it was probably all going to happen again; tonight, tomorrow night, the next night. It always happened late at night, a shameful, secret thing, too dark and terrible for open day.

One afternoon in early October we came home to find Mrs. Nagy and Mrs. Kaplan bustling around the kitchen and Fannie Herman standing in the hallway wringing her hands. Mrs. Nagy gave us a piece of strudel and told us brusquely to go down and stay in the street until our father came home. We hung around the stoop feeling uncomfortable, lost. We had to go to the toilet, we were getting cold in the falling light, we didn't feel like playing. Something was happening to our mother and why couldn't we see her? It had to do with her belly and the baby. I wanted to watch and at the same time wanted to be far, far away; to be someone else in another place, a girl who lived in a book.

When our father arrived and asked us what we were doing in the street so late, my brother mumbled something about the baby and we ran upstairs. We could hear Mrs. Kaplan's voice in the far big bedroom as my father walked into it and closed the door. Mrs. Nagy was in the kitchen putting stuffed cabbage and pieces of cornbread on the table. Our father called to us to eat and do our homework in the kitchen, he would eat later. We were to be quick and quiet and go to bed—and close the door—as soon as we were through. We didn't talk, as we often did, in bed; there was no point at which to start a discussion of something so large and forbidding, and words might betray our fear.

During the night we were awakened by a shriek and then another. Our door was pushed shut and we knew we were not to open it, not to get out of bed, not to see what was happening. People bustled in the hallway, to and from the kitchen, to and from the bathroom. Someone rang the doorbell and was admitted, probably the doctor. Through the sound of feet and the hushed voices, another scream and more, louder, more piercing, like ambulances. This I, too, had done to my mother, distorted her good-natured, singing person into a howling animal. I imagined her hair wild and swept across her staring green eyes, her pretty mouth torn by the screams, the doctor pushing the immense pincers into her belly and searching, searching for the baby, ripping her to pieces as my birth had done. My brother was asleep or pretended to be. I was alone in a guilt that made me want to disappear, to die.

Not knowing how to die, I separated myself from myself, one girl not there, one girl going through familiar actions in a dumbness and deafness like a thick rubber Halloween mask. I don't know who gave us breakfast; I ate it. I don't know what happened in school; I was there and managed to perform whatever was asked of me. I did my homework; it was correct. They told me I had a little sister; I didn't say anything. The women on the street asked me how my mother was; I said all right. This went on, the living in a cold, flat country, for several days, the guilt pushed down, out, away, and kept away. When my mother called to me from her bedroom to come and see the new baby, it was pretty, I called back, "Tomorrow," and ran to the street.

One of the days when my mother was still in her bed and we still fed by the neighbors, a monitor came into my classroom and handed a note to the teacher. We all sat up, eager for whatever news it might bring, an injunction from the principal about noise in the auditorium, an announcement of a shortened school day, possibly. My teacher called me to her and told me that I was wanted by my brother's teacher. All the kids stared as I walked awkwardly (was my skirt hitched up in back? my socks falling?) out of the room. When I reached his classroom, my brother was standing at her desk, looking shamefaced but not especially stricken. His teacher, Miss Sullivan, one of the smiling young ones, said she knew my mother had just had a baby but a big girl like myself could take care of a little brother almost as well as his mother could. But maybe I was too busy to notice that he didn't wash too well. Pulling his collar away from his neck, she showed me a broad band of dirt that began at a sharp edge just below his clean jaws. I had said every morning, "Wash your face," but forgot to mention his neck. Everything became hard and clear, as if it were cut out of metal, in that room, as deeply indelible as the painting of the boys listening to Sir Walter Raleigh's adventures in the auditorium: Miss Sullivan's blond lashes, her left eye a little bigger than the right, the spot of spit at the corner of her dry lips, the gray clouds of old chalk marks on the blackboard, the word cards, SENT, WENT, BENT, on the wall, the gluey tan wood of the windowsill, the pale afternoon sun streaking the floor, a red

sweater and a brown sweater hanging crooked in the half-open
wardrobe, the brown desks on iron legs, on each desk hands
folded as for a somber occasion like a visit from the nurse, above
each desk eyes staring at me.

I stood there leaden with shame until Miss Sullivan dismissed
me with, "See that he washes better," and sent me back to my
classroom. It was difficult to open the door and walk into those
eyes that were going to stare at me and later, at three o'clock,
come closer to ask what happened. I answered, "Oh, nothing.
Miss Sullivan wanted me to check my brother's homework; he's
careless, she said." I wanted to vomit, to stamp, to scream, to
break, to kill: him, me, them, my mother, my father, everything,
the whole world. But I had to walk him home. He searched my
face as he ran across the playground toward me, hesitated, and
attached himself to Jimmy, walking near me, as he had to, but a
safe distance away, on the far side of Jimmy. As soon as he
dropped his books on the floor of our bedroom he ran into my
mother's room, where I heard them giggling together. She called
to me, "Don't you want to come and see the baby?" I yelled back,
"Tomorrow," still afraid of what I might see, a baby with a ditch
in its head, a mother all rags of flesh, an exploded, splashed
cartoon animal. All my fault. My brother came back into the
kitchen where I was trying to peel an apple in one long coil, an
especially delicate operation because I was using a big breadknife.
He pushed my arm, breaking the coil, and ran toward the hallway, laughing. I threw the knife at him and saw it quivering in
the wall where his head had been a second before. It fell from the
wall. I picked it up and continued cutting the apple as I listened to
him screaming to my mother, "She tried to kill me! She threw the
knife, the big knife, at me! She's crazy! Send her away! Please,
Mama, send her away! I'm afraid of her!" I heard her slippers
patter down the hall, closed my eyes tight shut, and waited. She
shook me. "Open your eyes. Look at me." I looked, I would have

to sometime, and saw her as she was most mornings, in her thick brown bathrobe, her short hair not yet combed, her lips pale. "What's the matter with you? Do you know you could have killed him? Do you know that he would be dead, forever dead? Never talk again, never walk, never see, never hear? Do you know that you would be locked away in an asylum for crazy people? And spend the rest of your life, many, many years, with other crazies?" I said nothing, tried not to be there. "I've got to go back to bed now and attend to the baby. This your father will hear about and I won't get in his way. Whatever punishment you get you'll deserve."

It rained that evening and my brother was granted the privilege, usually mine, of carrying the umbrella to the El station. It was a special pleasure, a special ceremony, to go out into the wet night as if on an emergency mission—a nurse, a doctor—to rescue our fathers. We clustered, at the bottom of the steep El stairs, admiring the dark shine of the trolley tracks, the rain bubbling the puddles like boiling black cereal, holding the handles tight as the wind fought our umbrellas, listening to the rumble and roar of the train, the screeching stop, the rush of feet down the stairs. For many of us, the big smile as we yelled, "Pa, here I am, here," and were recognized and patted on the arm or head was the only overt affection we knew from our fathers. The umbrellas, now taller and single, separated to walk on their two long legs and their two short up Tremont Avenue, down to Bathgate, or shadowed themselves under the struts and tracks of Third Avenue.

By the time my brother and father got home and the wet umbrella placed in the bathtub, the story of the knife had been told, so serious a matter that it came before supper. Asked why I had thrown the knife, I answered—and it seemed a feeble reason— "Because his neck was dirty and he made me ashamed in front of his whole class." I couldn't say, "Because I hate mothers and babies and screaming in the night and people being pulled out of bellies with instruments and brothers who jump around and play while I have to take care of them." I couldn't find the words or shape the sentence because they were truly crazy things to say, worse than throwing knives. There was no preliminary lecture, cause and effect clear and simple. With a few words to my mother about the *gilgul*, the restless, evil spirit I must have in me— although he didn't really believe in such superstitious things—my father pushed me into the bathroom and, while he carefully pulled his belt out of the trouser loops, told me to lie across the covered toilet, pick up my skirt, and pull down my bloomers.

I had been slapped, on the face, on the behind, punched by boys and pinched by girls; my knees were often scraped, my fingers blistered and cut, but there was no preparation for the pain beyond pain of this first beating, the swish of the strap becoming a burning scream through my whole body, my arms shaking as they clung to the edge of the bathtub, my fingers scratching at the squealing porcelain, my ribs crushed against the toilet lid. I shrieked and begged, "Papa, don't. Stop, please. Please stop. Please, Papa." He stopped when he was out of breath, his face red, his brown eyes bulging. Replacing his belt, he walked out of the bathroom, closing the door. I stood there for a long while, then splashed cold water on my behind, fixed my clothing, and stood some more, not knowing where to go. In time I heard fumbling at the doorknob and my mother's voice telling my brother to get away, to let me be. A few minutes later she opened the door to tell me it was time to eat. I slipped out of the bathroom and into my bedroom, pushed the big chair against the door that had no lock, piled my books, my brother's books, the wooden sewing machine cover, and the heavy coats that were in the closet on the chair, and got into bed, pushing myself way, way down under the featherbed, stroking and rubbing myself until I fell asleep.

The next morning my brother banged on the door for his

books. As I pulled the heavy chair away so he could get in, I noticed his neck was clean. My mother was back in bed with the baby I had no intention of seeing. I grabbed a roll from the breadbox in the kitchen and ate it as I dressed, then left the house quickly, passing my brother, who stood on the third floor waiting at Jimmy's door. We avoided each other for the next day or two, he hanging on to Jimmy, I watching that they looked each way down the street before they crossed broad, busy 180th.

After my mother had spent her traditional ten days in bed, she put on the clothing she wore before the big belly and fixed us nice lunches: noodles, pot cheese, and raisins with cinnamon and sugar, radishes and cucumbers in sour cream, salami sandwiches. Ordinariness washed, day by day, over our lives except for the baby lying in my mother's lap in the kitchen. She looked unfinished and wandering, making strange faces, her eyes a milky blue and bobbling in her head, the tiny fingers reaching and curling toward everything, nothing. When her eyes turned to gold and steady, and some of the grimaces became smiles, I began to like her a little and let her pull at my fingers and hair.

8

Coney and Gypsies

Our baby sister was in a perverse way a great boon. She was frail, easily caught cold, had pinworms that had to be purged, which sometimes made her sicker, and was a troubled teether. With each tooth she had a fever and cried a lot. The first doctor we ever saw in our house—the obstetrician came and went behind our closed bedroom door; Dr. James was a fast-moving black shadow—was called in for the baby several times. It must have been an affluent time to afford doctors' visits, a time when my father brought home fairy-princess shoes to decorate. The extra piecework money he made was also spent for two summer weeks in Coney Island when my sister was nine or ten months old, teething and sickish all the time. Sea air was what the baby needed, my mother kept saying. After all, hadn't she cured us of whooping cough by spending days with us on the Staten Island ferry? And Coney Island wasn't so expensive and my father could come out a couple of times a week maybe and have all day Sunday on the beach and the boardwalk.

It was arranged, and after royal farewells to our less fortunate friends, the rich consoling and soaring over their poor relatives, we dragged the baby's crib and our bundles to El Dorado, the house in Coney Island, a ramshackle wooden place with a big porch. The several vacationing families like us each had one room crammed with two or three beds and clothing hooks on the walls. There was one community toilet and one large kitchen in which all the women cooked, whether separately or together I never found out. (That sort of summer living, whether at the beach or in the legendary "mountains," was known as a *kuch alein,* cook for yourself, the cheapest way to give one's children fresh air and escape for a week or two some of the exigencies of marriage.) The baby must have been quite sick because my usually careful mother let us loose on Coney Island every day for two weeks. After a breakfast of cold cereal with a couple of other children at one of the kitchen tables and a visit to the toilet, with two or three lunch nickels tied in a handkerchief knotted to a shoulder strap of my bathing suit, and instructions not to go too far into the water, not to buy candy with our lunch money, and to be back for supper at six, we were off.

We fought little or not at all during those weeks, too happy to want anything but what was: walking long streets staring at old people nodding on porches, at two kids with braces on their legs (the sea air was recommended for children with polio), who hopped up and down the stairs of one house like crooked birds, at the brilliant beach balls and shovels like derricks in shops on the boardwalk, at the machine in one shop that folded and kept folding skeins of taffy, at the fat plopping people and skinny stick people, at the white-skinned with red masks of sunburn, at the negro grasshopper children leaping and flying on their faraway street. It was a dazzling new world, like those in the movie travelogues that closed with, "As the sun sinks slowly in the west . . . ," and it was all ours. When it grew hot, we walked over to the sea and dared each other to go farther and farther out into the water. Both of us were several times dragged out in the undertow and grabbed by adults who demanded, "Where's your mother? Why doesn't she watch you?" and thrust us back on shore. After daring and daring more, being thrown and twisted, blinded and deafened by the water, shouted at by frightened and annoyed strangers, we became more cautious by silent accord and spent more time making sand castles and burying each other "up to the neck, keep away from my mouth and ears." We were both eager to spend the lunch money as soon as we left our house, and did it the first day, but learned to be patient after hours of hunger pangs. Lunch was a five-cent hot dog at any of dozens of stands, loaded with sauerkraut and, if we had an extra nickel, an ear of corn out of a big steaming cauldron. Dividing it was difficult: it didn't always break into two just halves, a meticulously observed principle, so we tried other solutions; one of them meant counting the rows of kernels, and if they were even, he crunched two rows and I the next two, and so on. If that didn't work out justly, the loser sucked on the cob, or got to lick the paper of a melting Baby Ruth on those days we decided against corn. Popcorn should have been easier, but counting out kernels, one for you, one for me, was too time-consuming for something we didn't care that much about, so we let it go. The tacit goal was to live as peaceably as we could in this paradise, "with liberty and justice for all," the Snake of Contention tied in his tree.

We found the Gypsies. They came through our Bronx streets from time to time, two or three women in big swinging skirts like colored winds, dusty long black hair, flashing gold teeth, and bold hands that demanded money, unlike the quivering old bums who bashfully begged. We were told to avoid them; they were filthy, they were thieves, and they kidnapped children. Our Coney Island Gypsies sat in a store behind a draped entrance, just off the boardwalk. The front of the shop was decorated with a naked head marked off in sections, probably for "studying bumps," which I had heard about from Helen Roth's big sister. Next to the cut-up head were a hand with lines on it and a watery picture of a glassy ball. Over the entrance, FORTUNES TOLD. COME RIGHT IN. We spent a good deal of time examining the head, the hand, and the glassy ball, trying to figure out how they told fortunes. Did a bump on the front slice of the head mean rich or smart? Could the glass ball show you a picture of whom you would marry? The lines on the hand, maybe they showed who would work hard, like the men who carried coal to the cellar, and who would have a soft job, like a teacher or librarian. All the fortune-telling we knew was a pick board crammed with little papers that, for a penny, could be poked out and unfolded to tell us, "You will marry rich," "You will be a success," "You will travel"—dumb things, we said; not altogether incredible, we thought. But this was the real goods, arcane, high-class fortune-telling that required mysterious charts and globes and the strange wisdoms of women in long red and pink satin skirts.

As we stood one day, edging toward the side of the draped doorway, a young woman in a long skirt and earrings like chandeliers came out and said, in recognizable English, "Hello. You're here again. Want some cake?" We were afraid and as usual much more afraid to confess fear. After hesitating, feeling shy, poking each other in and out of the doorway, we entered, looking for the cake. It was there, big and covered with chocolate icing, on a folding table, near it an older glittering Gypsy lady holding a knife. She gave us large chunks and cups of black tea with a lot of sugar. Was this the way they poisoned children to take them away, inert and senseless? Between small bites of the cake I waited for a numbed tongue, dizziness, pains in my stomach, anything ominous. I felt fine and my brother was doing well, babbling about our family and the sick baby and we had to take her here to the healthy air and we lived in the Bronx and he couldn't shut up. The young woman told the older one who had cut the cake what my brother was saying in her language—Romany, she explained—and invited me to sit down on a long low cushion if I wanted to. I sank to the purple and green flowers of the cushion, feeling as if I were floating, and accepted another piece of cake. While my brother continued entertaining the ladies, who smiled at him and each other broadly, I looked around. It was the most beautiful place I had ever been in. On the walls were intricately woven mazes of deep colors, little flowers and leaves caught in boxes of dark blue and red. Near these hangings were long spills of sky-blue satin. Other than the small table and two chairs there was no furniture, only cushions, heaps of them in brilliant colors and patterns. Near the back of the store, more and more like an Arab tent in the movies, there was an open cabinet of dark wood, carved as delicately as the shoes my father carved, on one of its shelves the glassy ball pictured outside. One lamp of metal with hundreds of little holes in it spread soft spots of light like stars. Sounds and smells of cooking came from behind a far curtain, but I never saw that room.

We didn't know when to leave, what the polite way of being with Gypsies was, so we stayed talking and staring, until the older woman said it was probably time to go home, our mother must be expecting us. Nothing was ever said about the Gypsies at home, though we went there frequent afternoons, always hanging around outside, near the skull and hand, waiting to be noticed and invited in. Sometimes we were offered sandwiches instead of cake, not too disappointing because we assumed that the strange meat in the sandwiches was ham or pork, of rarer value than cake. Sometimes the purple door drapes were folded together for a long time. That meant a customer and we tiptoed away, aching to peek through the folds to see Gypsy magic. We didn't dare risk the anger of the black-haired, black-eyed queens with the gold chains and earrings. They might yet hit us or poison us and sell us to other Gypsies.

The afternoon we said our last good-bye in Coney Island, the older woman, who had shown a great interest in the baby's teething and fevers, gave us a bone ring attached to a twisted, hornlike piece of coral, saying it was a teething ring, the coral attached for good luck. If our baby bit on it, she would feel much better and make nice strong teeth, too. I thanked her and thanked her again, nodding to be emphatic and to show I understood as she put the ring into my hand. We said good-bye—no kissing, no hugging, no handshaking, a great relief. As we walked home my brother asked to see the ring and, turning it around and around, decided it was old, used, and maybe full of germs. (It was old, used, and probably an antique that I regret not having saved.) We couldn't take it home, couldn't tell where we had gotten it. Even if we said we had found it, my mother would have thrown it away. So we dropped it into a sewer opening and forgot it.

The two weeks of freedom and being Gypsy children were not as easily forgotten. There was still a month before school started and we ran wild. The block wasn't enough anymore, even the empty lot. We snooped in the Italian market, a hundred times bigger than the local greenstores and butchers, hung with walls of salamis and cheeses like big clubs tied with ropes, all the way up on 183rd Street and Arthur Avenue. We skated far along Tremont to stare down on the tracks below Park Avenue, peering far downtown as we waited for trains that never seemed to run. But there was good garbage on the tracks, the rare sight of dozens of whiskey bottles along with the more familiar rotten oranges, old shoes, and mice rustling in torn bags of bread crusts and chicken bones.

It didn't last; we knew it wouldn't. We burst in, disheveled and streaked with dirty sweat, late one evening after our father had arrived. He ordered us into the bathroom to wash and comb our hair, declaring that we had become animals in Coney Island, it was time we were better controlled. My mother said nothing, but after that she took us and the baby, who was somewhat easier, to the park every afternoon to play quietly within her vision. I didn't mind, I read. But it was hard for my brother to live in circumscribed space, although he tried after our mother shouted him back from a game of Indians and Cowboys, himself both Indian and Cowboy, tracking fast and far.

During the hottest days we took off for Orchard Beach after an hour of scurrying preparation: Where are your bathing suits, put them on; put the bananas into the big shopping bag; I wonder if the eggs are hard-boiled yet; put your shirts and pants on over your bathing suit; Katie, run down to the grocery and buy six rolls, there's money on the table; don't put on those shoes, wear your old sneakers; not that dress, wear the blue one; hold the baby while I take the eggs out; take her bottle of milk out of the icebox and wrap it in a diaper so it won't get too warm; wrap up the towels in the old blanket and tie some string around it; leave the grapes alone, we'll need them on the beach when we're thirsty; here, the eggs are ready, wrap them up with the farmer cheese. Are we ready? Everything in the shopping bag? Did you put in your shovel? Hold the baby while I close the fire-escape window and lock the door.

My mother carrying the baby, my brother with the rolled blanket, and I with the shopping bag went to Tremont Avenue to wait for the summer trolley, a chariot of the gods served by Mercury. It clanged, it swayed, it screeched, and when its delicate wand slipped the wires in the sky, it shot little lightnings. Mercury got down from his daring ledge that ran the length of the trolley and coaxed the capricious wand that bent and quivered back to its wire. When he wasn't mastering electricity (at times, I thought, like a young, graceful Ben Franklin, without the spectacles and the moral wisecracks), our hero swung from open row to row, collecting fares, tapping change from the coin-shaped tubes on his chest, ripping transfers off a pad, one foot on his narrow ledge, one swinging in the air behind him, like Mercury, like a bird taking off.

We transferred to another trolley and yet another, riding into a place that had lawns around the houses and trees to screen them from the trolley tracks. We got off where the tracks were gritty and pulled our feet through the hot sand toward the water. It was never as crowded as Coney Island nor as interesting. We couldn't go into the water over our heads, we didn't eat hot dogs, only wholesome everyday food, we couldn't throw sand at each other because it might get into the baby's face. The sailboats in the distance were pretty to watch, dipping and straightening like ice skaters, and we argued about cloud shapes, was it a giant or a rhinoceros (surprising to find the same discussion in *Hamlet*). We carefully sucked and picked the threads off peach pits, preparing them for endless rubbing on the sidewalk to wear them down until they could be worn as rings, theoretically. (It took so long to make a peach ring, demanding much more patience than any of us had, that although reports kept coming in about magnificent rings on Monterey and on Arthur, we on Lafontaine never accomplished even one.)

It was nice on Orchard Beach, with the trolley rides, the big bag of food to dip into, the sailboats, the clouds, the water and watching it flow into the canals we dug near the water's edge, but it wasn't Coney Island; nothing ever again was.

9

Battles and Celebrations

In the fall, shapes became brisk, as sharp as the folds on new book covers. The hat factory smoke gathered itself together like long horses to ride the wind. The pale, weak forearms of our summer fathers disappeared under stiff dark cloth. Buildings began again to look like precise cutouts. The leaves fell from my tree and dried and turned in the gutter, making sounds like funeral veils. The jingling wagon of the ices man and its colored bottles disappeared. The icebox iceman put on his wool beanie with the pompom. Mrs. Katz closed the front window of her candy store and one could no longer buy from the sidewalk or hang out there as if one were going to buy, any minute. The gardeners in Crotona Park pulled out the red spikey flowers and gave them to us in big bunches. The *goyish* butchers hung the gray stretched-out bodies of hares in their windows. The kosher butchers heaped mounds of chicken fat to be rendered for use in Rosh Hashanah meals that celebrated the Hebrew New Year. Warm-skinned fruits gave way to cool apples and round purple Concord grapes appeared in slatted baskets in every greenstore, and Jews and

Italians on the block began to make wine. In a corner of every kitchen was a purple mess to which sugar was added and, I think, alcohol; it was watched and fed, attended to as if each family had a new baby. And, like a monstrous new baby, the wine stank up the street; it was a fleshy acrid smell, dark and dusty, and the end product that we sipped never seemed worth the trouble, the worried care. (Was I jealous of a small vat of spoiled grapes? Quite possibly. At times there seemed to be no limit to the greed for feeling jealous.)

Among the fall fashions that swept in on us from inventive Arthur Avenue, like making rings of dried peach pits, decorating the backs of our hands with cockamamies, soaking bubble gum in a glass of water overnight—as Joey's father did his false teeth—to make it hard and resistantly chewy the next morning, was that of embroidering, part of a *Little Women* phase, a time of maidenly dignity and refinement. We girls had small embroidery hoops, a few hanks of colored thread, and a stamped bit of cloth to work on. In for the sociability rather than the craft, a number of us settled for fast cross-stitching. When confronted with a leaf or flower, some would make a loop, catch it with a stitch at the end, and there it was, a petal. Those of us who, like myself, came from houses of dexterous, admired hands filled in the leaves and petals laboriously and with satisfaction as the spaces became shape and color, the cloth stippled with French knots and its edges tastefully tassled.

Ranged at the sides of the stoop stairs, six or eight of us sat like Old Country village women tatting or knitting in gossiping twilights. We let the gossiping go and sang and sang even when the light was too dim for sewing, outsinging the calls of our parents. We sang loudly at first, each voice outstriding the other. Shortly, an esthetic emerged; sad parts were sung heartbreakingly softly, jolly parts were sung jauntily but never coarsely shouted. We became divas, operatic actresses like Geraldine Farrar and

Rosa Raisa, capable of melting the cement sidewalk with "Because I love you, I've tried so hard but can't forget," with "Not for just an hour, not for just a day, not for just a year, But Always." We were seductive minxes, spit-curled soubrettes in "Does your mother know you're out, Cecilia? Does she know that I'm about to steal ya," a felicity of rhyme matched only by Henry Wadsworth Longfellow. We were quivering, freezing, starving old ladies when we whimpered "Over the hill, over the hill" on our way to the poorhouse. One of our most satisfying songs was a ballad that had wandered with pioneers and immigrants to settle, with small local variations, into many cities (one version, more recently heard as sung by Westchester girls, placed the action in Tarrytown; another *mise en scène* was Buffalo). Our version, sung with dreamy rue and gentle defiance, ran, as ballads do, to length. The truncated matter left by memory holds the bare bones of the story:

> *In Jersey City where I did dwell*
> *A butcher's boy I loved so well.*
> *He stole my heart away from me*
> *And sat another on his knee.*
>
> *He sat another on his knee*
> *Because she had more gold than me.*
> *Her gold will fade, her silver fly*
> *And then she'll be as poor as I.*

We were, of course, repeating the joy of singing in the school auditorium and, more remotely, repeating traditions of which we had no conscious awareness, echoing the group singing on the evening streets of villages in Russia, in Poland, in Hungary, in Italy, to which we were still intimately linked.

The fights of autumn in Apartment 5B, 2029 Lafontaine,

started with pencil boxes and rulers and went on to clothing for the New Year holidays. My brother didn't care; a new pair of pants meant staying clean and untorn, no marble shooting on his knees, no stickball and sliding to home base, a manhole cover in the middle of the horse-shit street. He would just as soon not, but he got them and suffered mildly. My growth was more erratic than his, all finished by the time I was eleven, a leaps-and-bounds development that left me bewildered and with clothing that never fit. To allow for lengthenings and broadenings like Alice in Wonderland, a new coat was bought two sizes too large, the sleeves covering my hands to the fingernails, the skirt almost to my ankles, and as poisonous as the cloak Medea sent her doomed rival Creusa. By the next year's holidays, the coat was tight across my back, the sleeves bared my wrists, the skirt was high above my knees, and the whole confection was as hideous as it had been the year before. I wore the coat when it was long, I wore it when it was short; I had no choice. But my mother and father had some sharp words on "humiliating" a growing girl, and what the devil did she mean by "humiliating"; wasn't the coat new or like new? Anyhow, she had no business indulging my *pianovi chasto* sensibilities. There were millions of children all over the world who didn't have a rag for their behinds, who were freezing in the streets of Russia or working, at my age, in the coal mines of Pennsylvania. They were off! And I took my misery to the fire escape, hoping I would catch double pneumonia in the wind and become as pale and thin as Bessie Love and almost die in a clean white hospital, my life saved by Wallace Reid, who told my father, straight out, not to be such a stingy louse and made him promise to reform. Otherwise, he, Wallace Reid, would go to the police and arrange to adopt me.

After the "Ohlly Nohly" sung by our black neighbors on 98th Street came other religious experiences on Lafontaine, one on a

Friday evening in November. The cookies baked that afternoon were in a covered dish on a high kitchen shelf beyond a child's reach, the kitchen smelled of gefilte fish and the rest of the house of lemon oil furniture polish, forever the smell of cleanliness. The wooden floors were slick and shining; there were freshly washed and starched curtains on the dining-living room windows. My mother had put two candlesticks on the big round dining table, lit them, and placed a white cloth on her head. She began to talk at them in the same singsong that Uncle David murmured when he bound his arm with black leather strips and swayed back and forth. It was talking to God, we had been told, and women did it only on Friday night, the only time God had for women. In the middle of a phrase my mother took off her headcloth, blew out the candles, and, turning to my astonished father, said—in Polish, which we still spoke sometimes—"No more. I never believed it, I don't now. And I don't have to do it to please my mother, or anyone, here." She never lit candles again, although Friday night kept its usual smells, shines, and crispness appropriate to the Eve of Wonderful Saturday the day of the movies, and later reenactment of our favorite bits, the girls snaking like vamps, the boys leaping up and down the stairs, thrusting and jabbing the air with sticks like the swords of Douglas Fairbanks.

Nor did our mother ever go to the synagogue on Arthur Avenue, except once or twice to hear my brother sing in the choir when she dragged me to join the women's section where the grandmothers held lemonlike fruits to their noses, meant to revive them should the Yom Kippur fast cause them faintness. It was insufferable to know that he earned two dollars for Passover and two dollars for the ten days of Rosh Hashanah-Yom Kippur. I could sing as true and loudly as he and could learn to make the Hebrew sounds as quickly, but they didn't—ever—take girls. It would be gratifying to suggest feminist passion in the resentment, but it dealt only with the stinker amassing two dollars and two dollars more, a fair advance toward a two-wheeler bike, while I earned nothing. Arithmetic, an abomination too, helped feed the angry fires: you could go to the movies twenty times for two dollars, or buy forty big five-cent ice-cream cones I could be distracted now and then from my brother's pile of gold on Yom Kippur. I liked Yom Kippur; there was something extreme, outrageous, about it, especially when the old men got angry with God. Passover was fun, seders with funny things on the table: baked bones, baked egg, a bitter mash, a sweet mash whose significance we were told and forgot in sipping wine and hunting for the hidden matzo. After we all sang "*Chad Gad Yoh*," something about a little goat in one of those songs that got bigger and bigger (like "Old MacDonald Had a Farm"), we were dumped on a pile of coats in the bedroom to lie in a nest, like birds, to sleep on warm clouds like Wynken, Blynken, and Nod. Passover meant *bubeluch*, plump matzo meal pancakes covered with sugar, and it meant, on rainy days when we took lunch to school, matzo smeared with chicken fat or, best of all, a cold scrambled egg between two slabs of buttered matzo. And then there was the great classic, *matzo brei*, pieces of matzo soaked in milk, squeezed into a delectable mess, and fried to golden curls and flakes—one of the dishes that evokes piercing darts of nostalgia in every Jewish breast and stories of childhood Passovers complete with lightly drunken uncles.

But with all its pleasures, Passover was only nice. Yom Kippur was weird, monumental. Imagine not eating for a whole day to prove something or other to God, or yelling at God in the synagogue as the bearded old men did in their white shawls, their heads thrown back, their Adam's apples tearing at their skinny throats. They made animal noises as their bodies whipped back and forth almost to the ground, their open mouths jerking their beards as they sang wildly of atonement and complaint. With a towel over my head, I practiced the urgent bending back and forth and making Hebrew sounds, but didn't get any feeling into it, or out of it, and no understanding. When I turned down oatmeal one Yom Kippur morning, announcing I was going to fast, my father said that in that case I shouldn't have had barley soup and boiled beef last night, the time to have started fasting. Anyhow, it doesn't count until you're thirteen and a boy, and anyhow, don't be crazy. Eat.

There was a certain enjoyable distinction and shame in being among the few Jews on the block who used the same utensil for both butter and meat dishes, blithely denying the Bible's injunction, as my father explained it, not to seethe lambs in the milk of their mothers. Why? He didn't know exactly. We never saw the forbidden shrimp and lobster; too expensive for anyone we knew, they presented no problem. Ham and pork were surrounded by trembling auras: the absolutely forbidden, made more repulsive by slabs of white lard like dead flesh and the smooth pink piglets like skinned babies grinning from the windows of butcher shops. Neither of my parents ate pork or bacon—my mother tried once when she was frying bacon for my sick sister and couldn't force the first bite into her mouth—simply because their upbringing and the millennia of ancestors, including Moses and the Prophets, thundered against the violation and paralyzed their mouths and throats.

Pretty, springy Miss Torrence asked me to buy a sandwich for her one rainy day; it was to be ham and cheese with lettuce and mayonnaise on white bread. I carried it back to school from the German delicatessen on 180th Street as if it were an explosive thing, away from my body, the bag held only by my thumb and forefinger, proud to have been given such a distinguished commission by one of the goddesses, heroic because I was risking God's displeasure. Carrying ham, its abominableness enhanced by being stuck to cheese, a milk dish, the forbidden esoterica folded together on elegant, neatly cut Tip-Top white bread, infinitely high-class compared to our thick slabs of rye or cornbread, made buying and delivering the sandwich just frightening enough, just forbidden enough, just confusing enough to be a glorious adventure.

While the fall and the Jewish New Year belonged to us, the winter belonged to the *goyim* and Christ, their closest relative, now only remotely ours because we had treated him so badly; stuck him on a pole with nails and cut open his side and made him drink vinegar. The customary American symbols of Christmas—the elaborately wrapped toys brought by Santa Claus and laid under a glittering tree, the green wreaths and red ribbons—were absent from the Italian houses. Instead of Christmas trees, the De Santises, the Silvestris, the Bianchis arranged little country scenes of farm animals and shepherds with crooks all looking up in admiration at the pretty blond lady with the new baby in her lap. The Bianchis also had beautiful little angels with long fingers like Good Fairies. They came all the way from Naples, Carla told me, brought by her silent grandmother, thin, austere, always dressed in black. No one, not even Carla, was allowed to touch them. The only house festivities, Maria Silvestri told me, was a lot of eating of fish on Christmas Eve and card playing and wine drinking when the men grabbed and pinched the women. Early in the morning, the women and the old men went to church to greet the newborn Christ, leaving the men and children who had come up from Mulberry Street sleeping all over the house, three and four in a bed.

Feeling a bit like a traitor and preening in my knowledge of a wider world, a witness to mysteries unknown to the other Jewish kids, I luxuriated in descriptions of what I had seen and been told of the Italian festivities. Given warm welcome in Italian houses mainly because my mother was available at all hours for emergency help and advice, my closest friends were Italian. I liked the

shouting and laughter, the plants in backyards, the bossy, powerful grandparents, and the thrilling disrespect with which Italian
mothers gave their kids wine with their lunchtime spaghetti so
that they spent the afternoon school sessions sleeping, heads cush-
ioned by arms folded on scratched wooden desks; fauns, children
of Bacchus sleeping off Dionysian revels, my favorite anarchists.

Resenting my intimacy with Marias, Carlas, and Caterinas,
the Ruthies, the Rosies, the Hannahs nibbled poisonously at me
and my *krist* friends. They had additional ammunition in the
obvious fact that our house was not kosher; my mother even gave
our baby bacon, pig meat, *pheh*! How could I eat an Italian apple
that lay in the icebox with pork? How could I play with dopes
who thought the same baby was born year after year, maybe for
as much as a hundred years, and decided he was God? And
weren't they drunks (quoting the axiom that all Gentiles were
drunkards, one of the feeble ripostes to anti-Semitism), sending
their kids to school reeling, full of wine? What kind of Jew was I,
anyhow? I didn't know. So I stopped displaying my ethnological
enlightenments and compartmentalized my life, on one side of
the street sort of Jewish, on the other sort of Italian, yet always
trying to arrange a comfortable melding: Italians were really sort
of Jewish, anyhow.

Besides the holiday, the tinsel like silver rain, in the five-and-
ten, and the fat Santa Claus that bent and blinked like a moron
from the window of the music store on Tremont Avenue, winter
meant a constant struggle over warm underwear. My tall green-
eyed goddess, Miriam Silverberg, the niece of the people next
door, and rich enough to wear braces on her teeth, wore high
knee socks all winter and no long underwear. When I pointed
this out to my mother, she countered with Miriam's age, four-
teen, and my miserably few years. Also, she wasn't Miriam's
mother, nor was Miriam's mine, and I had to do what the

mother with whom God had afflicted me said, and no more arguments. Tomorrow morning I was to put on long underwear, down to my ankles, and long stockings, pulled all the way up, attached to metal garters that hung from a cotton vest. For years, until I was old and strong enough to refuse to go to school so grotesquely dressed, I went through a stubborn ritual: out of the house in the morning, and into the cellar behind the furnace where I pulled down my stockings to become fat sausages twisted and rolled below my knees. Up went the underwear to make even fatter sausages about my thighs. Just before I got to school and snoopy teachers, as bad as mothers, the elaborate process was reversed. School out for lunch, down the stockings and up the underwear; around the corner from the house, down the underwear and up the stockings, and so on through eight changes each school day. Four fat rolls on baby-fat legs made awkward walking but I felt splendidly fashionable as the winds and winter rains froze my knees, and triumphant. *She* thought she had won, while, really, I had, my first experience of silent battles and silent victories.

I liked her much better late winter afternoons when we went to the butcher together and she smiled her small aristocratic Warsaw smile when the butchers made their coarse jokes aimed mainly at the country *yupkes* who came in bright-eyed and smirking. The men in broad, bloody aprons looked like giants, one with the bushy eyebrows of the huge cop in Charlie Chaplin films. The store was warm with light, with the glisten of entrails, of fat, of the big shining meat grinder and big hooks hung with livers and hearts that seemed still to be quivering, like live flesh, like the big bloody hands that cut and pulled and ripped carcasses apart. The warm, fatty air was full of the butchers' ringing voices: "Come, my beauties of Israel, my Esthers, my Shebas, take what I've got—and have I got!" "You want breast? Me, too, I want breast, *tsotskele* [cutie]." While he sawed up marrow bones (a delicacy, incidentally, that belonged to our father exclusively) or ground beef that came out like red worms, one of the men would tell the story of a butcher who suspected a woman of stealing a chicken and stuffing it into her blouse. The butcher quickly reached in to encounter an innocent featherless breast, and being a witty fellow, like all butchers, asked calmly, "Already plucked?" The men roared, the women tittered.

Never quite sure of how much Yiddish we understood but suspecting it was enough for dirty jokes (the reason our parents began to tell their jokes in Polish, which we children had mostly forgotten), my mother sent me out of the store to wait in the street as the spirits grew high and salacious. I didn't mind too much, if it was snowing. The street lamps were rippled like ballerinas' skirts and it was lovely to see the snowflakes come out of the dark sky, brighten along the ripples, glow for a second or two in the full light, float down to darkness and melt, a ballet to music too delicate to hear.

Visits to the butcher shop were only pauses, periods of détente, in the "you'll catch a cold" battles. One constant battle concerned itself with wearing rubbers, which still strangle, as throttled fury strangled me then. I wouldn't wear rubbers because they were ugly, a nuisance to take off and put on, and an impediment to the trials of endurance I was launched on. My father would complain that I was eating up his life by ruining my shoes, my mother would warn that I was inviting pneumonia and would have to go to the hospital where people died, but I had to try to endure the icy slush that seeped into my shoes, gathered in my stockings, and froze my feet blue and painful. As I had to climb the two-story rocks behind the hat factory (and made it a couple of times), egged on and sneered at by the practiced boys who flew ahead of me.

One solution to the rubbers controversy was to tear out of the house without them, clattering down the stairs while my mother called after me to come back, reenacting a Tobie-Fannie Herman scene. My frenzied Tobie flight and my mother's suddenly shrill Fannie-voice always return when weather and reason, fighting passionate unwillingness, force me into a shop to try on overshoes or even sleek waterproof boots. They fit. Yet they strangle, as they did in childhood, and I give them away, self-doomed to dragging ruined shoes and blue feet through icy slush for the rest of my life.

10

Jimmy and Death

Jimmy Petrides, my brother's best friend from the time we moved to Lafontaine Avenue when both boys were about five, was lank and had a neat face, as if someone had made a careful drawing of it before he was born; the lines of his thin eyebrows and thin nose straight, the lower line of his eyes straight, and the arches above as complete and round as the pretty hollow at the back of his neck. Like all the other boys he leaped and bellowed in the street but he was quiet and shy when he came to our house on rainy or cold days to make trains of boxes or spools and to match baseball cards with my brother. Although they lived in our house, two stories below us, we knew very little of his family. His father was one of the many anonymous men in caps with paper bags under their arms who rushed to the El in the morning and came back more slowly at night. Jimmy had a younger sister whom he began to take to school when he was about eight, a dark-gold little girl who clutched his hand and wouldn't talk to anyone else. Once home from school, she stayed in her house; we rarely saw her on the street even as she grew older. Mrs. Petrides was also rarely visible and wonderful when she was, a silent solitary thing like a tree alone in a field. There may have been other Greek families on the block but not in our immediate houses, and she had very few English words to exchange with her neighbors. Nevertheless, families in immigrant neighborhoods being inevitably interdependent, for shopping advice, for medical information, for the care of each other's children and the exchange of kitchen delicacies, Mrs. Petrides was offered strudel by Mrs. Nagy, the *Ungarische dripke* who was the best baker on the block. Big, clumsy Mrs. Kaplan, the loudest behemoth of the house, took her a length of *kishka* (stuffed intestine), her specialty, which Jimmy told us they couldn't eat; all that rubbery stuff. My mother's contribution was to ask Jimmy if his mother would like to go to the English classes with her, explaining that they were held during afternoon school hours and she would be back before three o'clock. He said, "She won't, she's too ashamed," the word for embarrassed or shy. There must have been a number of women like Mrs. Petrides on the block, who had no one to speak with when the husband and children were away, no one to ask where she could buy feta cheese or Greek oil. Tall and slender, with Jimmy's long eyebrows and straight nose, her sandy hair in a long full knot at the back of her head, her high-arched eyes fixed straight ahead, she looked like a lady on the front of a storybook ship, as strong and as lonely.

My mother and the other women said that if Mrs. Petrides had taken them into her house to see Jimmy when he got sick—it didn't need words—or had asked the De Santis boys to take him to Fordham Hospital, Jimmy might not have died. We never found out the cause of his death; children were told about the deaths of the old but never of children, a knowledge too dreadful to speak. The first intimations of Jimmy's illness came from my brother, who was hanging around one rainy October day being mean and restless. He got in my mother's way as she was trying to boil diapers in the steaming cauldron on the stove; he woke our little sister, who had been sick and was napping; he hid my brand-new pencil with the removable cap eraser. My mother suggested he go down to play in Jimmy's house or ask him to come up. He said Jimmy was sick, he hadn't gone to school that day. The next day and the next when he was asked if Jimmy had been in school he again answered, "No," and although the weather had cleared, he refused to go down into the street. He pushed spools and boxes around for a while, read for a while, colored a picture with the baby for a while, but mostly he hung around, like a tired little old man.

The whole house was quiet. The women didn't talk much; only Tobie Herman clattered noisily up and down the stairs. My mother must have known that Jimmy was dying, but I knew nothing until my brother burst into the house crying as neither my father with his beatings nor I with my fierce teasing could make him cry. His face was broken, tears pouring down his sweater, his fists clenched and shaking as if he were fighting, his feet stamping. When we calmed him a little, though he still shuddered and wept, he told us that Mr. Petrides, home from the factory that day, came over to him and said that Jimmy was dead, that we would never see him again. "What does he mean, *never*? That I won't ever see Jimmy again? What does he mean?" and his heels stamped the floor and his fist punched the air again and the terrible crying started again. I wanted to console him, not quite knowing what to say, saying something while my mother held him on her lap, a big boy of nine who allowed the indignity because he was in terrible trouble.

That evening when my father came home he was still shuddering, lying on our bed with the baby, who offered him her doll and conversation. He didn't respond, which made her cry. That night he didn't eat, and he slept deeply, shuddering every once in a while. Like the street, school was hushed the next morning. The news of Jimmy's death, carried in whispers through the auditorium, in the playground, on the stairs, in toilets, was a funerary garland that wrapped itself around the whole red brick building. Street life stopped: no ball, no marbles, no ropes lashing at the sidewalk, no stickball, no fights, no singing on the stoop. The day of the funeral must have been Saturday, there was no school. We returned books to the library and picked out others early and quickly, then went home to clean up and wait, not knowing quite what we were waiting for. We had seen funerals in the movies, in the news, but they were of grand and old people, not of a boy, not on our street. It was a cool sunny day, the big garbage cans and the metal roof of the De Santis garage shining bright and hard. As we sat on the stoop we heard stirrings on the inside stairs. The inner door opened and two men came down into the small hall where the letter boxes were, carrying a long black box. My brother gasped and I dragged him down the block, looking back to see what was happening. After the box came Mr. Petrides in a black coat and Mrs. Petrides with a black veil over her head and falling down her black coat. Behind them a few more people in black, one of the women holding by the hand the little Petrides girl whose head, too, was covered with a black scarf. The box was carried slowly down the stoop stairs, into the gutter, and then, followed by the family, headed toward 180th Street. Telling my brother that funerals were quiet so he shouldn't make noise, I ran ahead to look at Mrs. Petrides from the sidewalk. She wasn't crying; she had died, too, with only the clear drawing of her features left on dull white paper.

As the family walked slowly, following the black box, held high by the four black arms like burned tree branches, the children began to trail after, led off by the two youngest De Santis boys, both in their early teens, and then the other Italian children, who seemed to know about funerals: Maria Silvestri and her brother Louis, Caroline and Petey Santini, the Bianchi kids. My brother ran into the gutter to join Petey, and I followed him, hesitating for a moment, to walk with Caroline. Awkwardly, hesitantly, the Jewish kids watching from the sidewalk began to walk with us, some of them kids who might later be hit for joining a *goyish* funeral. The two Ruthies came and Helen, Rachel, and Hannah, Sidney and Milton, the Sammies, the Izzys. My brother began to cry, quietly, and I went to him while Caroline took Petey, whose face had begun to quiver. More crying around me, behind me, growing louder and louder, coming out of twisted eyes, leaking into open mouths. (Those weeping faces combine inextricably in my memory with the image of the mourning cherubim of Giotto, wailing as they hover over the body of Christ.)

I couldn't understand why they were all crying. My brother, yes, Jimmy had always been his very best friend and he liked him more than anyone else in the world, more than our mother. The other boys had liked him too, an easy, gentle boy who yielded to them rather than fight. But why were the girls crying over a Greek boy they had hardly ever played with? What did they know about death that I didn't? What were they seeing? What were they feeling? Like them, I knew dead people were put in a hole in the ground and covered with earth. Were they crying because the earth might choke him, because he might open his eyes in the dark, alone, screaming, and no one to hear him? Maybe then he would really, truly die. Was that what they meant by "frightened to death"? As a Christian boy he should become an angel. Was there a saw in the coffin to cut through the black wood and a shovel to dig away the dirt? And once out, how long would he have to stand in the dark alone before God sent the blond lady with the naked baby down through the windy night clouds to carry him back up with her?

Seeing sick Jimmy standing alone, waiting—for how long?—to be rescued from the dark made me cry as fully, with my whole body, as I couldn't on Third Avenue in the dark, when I was five. Maybe my brother was crying the same memory: in a dark, unknown place, lost, unprotected. We were crying for the same reason that we hid our heads in the movies when a child wandered alone, that we quickly skipped pages when a book threatened to tell about an abandoned child. (Maybe we were also crying, like the women who went to the movies "to enjoy a good cry," for the relief not too often permitted us.)

By the time we reached 180th Street, my mother had caught up with us. Taking us each by the hand, she said she didn't think they would let us into the Greek church and certainly not into the cemetery; come home, stop crying. We ate, we slept, we went to school, we asked no questions. One of the block chroniclers said the Petrides family had gone back to Greece, another said they moved downtown near cousins who had a stable. We were no longer interested in the family—the godlike child's gesture of quickly dissolving away anything that wasn't immediately attached to our ears, our eyes, our greeds, our envies. Our fears hung on for a while. No one mentioned Jimmy. His name was a black omen, a sign that children could die, and as fast as we could, we obliterated his name, too.

The Halloween after Jimmy's death was a brutal time. When the slashing dark rains of late fall came on Halloween, I was glad to stay at home. On clear nights I was impelled to go, curious, defying my reluctance and fear. The only children in costume— no witches, no gypsies, no pumpkin heads, no pirates—were small wandering foreign bands stumbling in their fathers' old pants, tottering on the crooked high heels of mothers' shoes. They did not invade houses to ask for "trick or treat," expecting apples or candy. Their collections were made on the street, accosting adults with "Got a penny, mister?" The pickings on Lafontaine were poor; this was begging, and begging was the ultimate disgrace, contemptible even for kids. Furthermore, there weren't too many spare pennies around, and those had to be saved for a stick of gum, a string of licorice for one's own kids. We were impressed and wary of their boldness, these invaders from Washington, Bathgate, and Third Avenue with their threatening, demanding hands, and when we saw them coming, moved step by step backward to the top of our stoops, ready to disappear into the inner halls.

It was an evening of mayhem for the bigger boys on our street, joined by a couple of their heroes from Arthur Avenue. They wheedled long black stockings, a color and shape of magic and malevolence, from mothers who were ignorant of their use that night and were too careless or busy to ask. The stockings were filled with flour or chalk carefully collected from schoolroom discards and pounded into white powder. They became whip sausages to beat legs, leaving white clouds on stockings and flesh. Nothing serious, a mark of being with the daring on this night, a good time for displaying agility in jumping, turning, running, avoiding the whips. A more vicious invention, automatically blamed on the Italian and Irish boys, was to fill the stocking with unbroken pieces of chalk or, lacking enough of those, ash, coal, and small rocks. To the game of hunter and prey was added the exciting element of real injury, a young perverse version of Russian roulette: which whip would only mark, which whip would bruise or crack a bone?

That especially violent night, the big bellowing boys twirling the black whips over their heads like cowboys' lariats, like frenzied dervishes, I decided to get out of the fun that was not fun and turned my back to run up the stoop stairs and home. A sharp blow hit my calf, throwing me on the top step. I looked at my leg. Something completely impossible was happening to it: a thin spurt of blood was coming through my stocking, straight as an arrow. I knew blood dripping from a scraped knee, a cut finger, a bleeding nose, but never in a thin fast burst like this, straight out into the air. When it slowed, after moments when I saw my life leaving me very quickly, to a dripping trickle, I went upstairs and into the bathroom. My mother was reading yesterday's English paper in the kitchen, and my father was busy with the piecework he had set up in the dining-living room. No one asked any questions. I washed the bloody stocking and my leg, given plenty of time for a careful examination of my calf, which showed only a puncture like a mosquito bite, by my brother's arrival. He was covered from head to foot, a ghost boy, in layers of chalk and soot, ordered into the hall to slap it off before he came into the house again. Then take a bath. It wasn't bath time, he protested, it wasn't Saturday; he wasn't dirty; he hated baths; it wasn't fair. My mother was implacable and called to me to start running water into the tub, and then to get ready for bed.

Alone in bed, I examined my calf again. There was only that tiny hole, hardly visible, but because my blood had jumped out of it in such a weird way, I knew I had a terrible blood disease. And would soon die, like the children with rare diseases reported by the Sunday *American*. My left calf became the focus of my life, never forgotten for a moment. The bruise turned strange colors, purplish streaked with a sick yellow like pus. It didn't hurt much, but my leg felt heavy, draggy, beginning to reveal diagnostic signs of the disease that would kill me. Some weeks before I had seen, in the Sunday *American* magazine section that Mr. Haskell left with the jokes, a drawing that filled most of a page: a woman carrying a little nude girl past a piece of sharp-edged furniture whose corner sent a chip of the child's buttock flying into the room. I read the article, mesmerized, memorizing each detail. First one affected area turned white and hard and then another. The child gradually turned to stone, as immobile as a statue: an actual statue, dead, when her lungs and heart became marble. That was my disease. I poked my arms and legs; they felt cold and stiff and the white mark made by my finger took an interminable time to turn pink again. My legs moved sluggishly, as if I were dragging stone shoes. My eyesight was becoming misty and I had to bend deeper into my book to see. I wasn't hearing too well, either. My mother said I wasn't listening, not paying attention, and I wasn't. It took great concentration to avoid the sharp corner of the piano, not to bump against a dresser or a classroom desk, not to cause a chip to fly off my arm, my back, a sign of the end. Death was surely coming, but I was not yet ready for conclusive signs.

At night, lying next to my brother, who thrashed around in fight dreams muttering the dirty words he was not allowed to say during the day, listening to the gurgles of my sister wrapped in her baby cocoon of sleep, I pushed and felt my heavy cold body and tested my eyes by trying to pierce the dark. Was I seeing the hook on the door and the knob on the closet, or only remembering, as people going blind must? Would I hear the clatter of the milkman's bottles or imagine them? What would my brother do when he found me motionless with white stony eyes one morning soon? What would my mother say? What would she do? Would everyone follow my box, crying, as when Jimmy died? Since I couldn't become an angel like Christian children, I would lie in the box, smelling myself rot, hearing the flesh fall off my bones, feeling my eyes roll out of my head and my hair creep down to my shoulder bones. At one moment during one of those dying nights the stoicisms I had been practicing, maybe to this end of suffering and dying without a murmur and alone, left me. I found myself running down the hall to my parents' bedroom. Their door was half open. I slipped through it and stood for a long time looking at them and listening to their breathing. They usually snored—a duet my brother and I imitated masterfully— but now there was no sound. I bent lower to listen to my mother's breathing, to watch her chest rise and fall. Nothing. My father's chest wasn't moving either, and there was not the faintest sound of breath. They had caught my disease and turned to stone. They were dead. I had given them my death.

I shrieked and both my parents sat up, sleepy-eyed and bewildered, as if they had come a long way and didn't know where they were. They asked me what had happened—was I sick? Was the baby all right? And my brother? I said nothing, not knowing how to think, what to say. On their repeated questioning I said I had a terrible bellyache. My mother got out of bed and took me to the bathroom for a large dose of the milk of magnesia that was always in the medicine cabinet. I took it eagerly and stayed home from school the next morning because I had to go to the bathroom a lot. By lunchtime I was hungry and ate a large bowl of rice boiled in milk, which was good for bellyaches, and went off to school, hoping I hadn't missed yet another complication of percentages, an impenetrable subject. By what means I made a miraculous recovery, escaping imminent death, transferring my death to my parents and their rejection of that death, the whole terrible matter capable of being dispelled in a fake bellyache and milk of magnesia, is difficult to explain. It was probably a swing in the vagrant, impassioned imaginings of childhood that plummet into black pits and fly into blossoming trees in dizzy alternations. At any rate my flesh bounced back pinkly when I poked it, my fingers became dexterous enough to weave a long string rope on a spool with four nails hammered into it, and I outran Miltie, something of a champ runner, in a race around the block.

11

Revelations

The spring I was ten and a half I was crazy with love: I was in love with Arthur, mostly because his name wasn't Sammy or Benny or Petey. He was so neat and tight, a clear, straight part in his plastered hair, a starched collar fresh every day, clean neck, clean ears. An Arrow Collar boy. He sat at the desk in front of me, and as if my eyes were tongues, I lapped and lapped at his perfection, his goyishness. Although he lived on the block, he was never part of the Saturday morning hordes that skated down Tremont Avenue to change books at the library, nor was he ever in the Saturday afternoon crowd in the movies. He never played in the street, nor did he walk to school with us; his mother took him there, called for him at lunchtime, walked him back, and called for him again at three o'clock. Though we were in the same class, the same seats, for five months, I never spoke to him or he to me. At this long sour remove, it seems I should have resented his mother's protection against us, the flying kids with the falling socks, but at that time I considered her exquisite care a mark of his distinction, no more than a prince deserved.

I was in love with Mrs. Bender, the teacher who stroked her large smooth breasts as she read "Hiawatha," her hand moving with the rhythm of "By the shore of Gitche Gumee,/By the shining Big-Sea-Water." I was in love with the "Bacchanale" from *Samson and Delilah*, which we would put on the Victrola and whoop and holler and thump to while my mother laughed. I was in love with Mrs. Polanski's new poodle, white and round as a snowball, with a dirty ass. I was in love with the sadness of "All Alone" and the tearful wit of the last line of "Remember": "But you *forgot* to remember." I was in love with consumption, the artistic, graceful wasting that inspired Chopin. When my mother walked into the street in her new brown suit and beaver hat on the first day of Passover, she was so beautiful that I couldn't see her; her radiance blinded me. My brother, in spite of our steady urge to mutual mayhem, appeared all gold and dazzling as he played stickball in the street. And I was in love with me, grown suddenly taller and thinner, and I had, I was sure, what they called in poems a swan neck. I was as complete and smooth as a fresh pea pod.

Above all, I was in love with Helen Roth. She was bigger and older than I, broad-boned, fleshy, tough. She answered back to teachers, her mother, our mothers, who called her "*pisk*," Big Mouth. Awed by the fact that her mother sent her to the delicatessen—too expensive for most of us—to pick out whatever *she* wanted, I went there with her often to wonder at the profligacy with which she ordered and to be deeply moved by her talent for eating a whole hot red pepper without blinking or coughing. And she came equipped with an older brother, who went to high school and was distant and beautiful, and a big sister, who went to work, elegant, fancy, in shining high-heeled pointed shoes.

I adored Helen for having the monumental courage to be left back in school. My father would have killed me, beaten me to death. Or I would have run away to die in some distant cellar.

Here *she* was, waving her dooming report card with an airy, untroubled gesture worthy of Gloria Swanson.

Helen's most admirable role, though, was that of friend and messenger to her neighbor, the skinny, trembling Mr. Ricciardi, the cellist with the thick glasses, for whom she organized secret little parties. Sunday mornings when his mother was in church, he sent Helen to gather three or four of her friends; no Italian girls, he said; they spoiled the fun, he said. I went once. She gathered us up with whispers and led us on, eager and excited, to the bakery on Tremont Avenue. There we bought rare gems of chocolate-mounded, pink-iced, custard-filled cakes that never quite came to two dollars Helen carried; Mr. Ricciardi had said she could keep the change, she told us. It was her honor to carry the pastry box, dangling it high and showily, to trouble the other kids not invited to the party. We walked quietly up the three flights of 2027, Helen first, as leader and to make sure her parents' door was closed, then we slipped into the Ricciardi apartment. It was close and dark as a cave. I could dimly make out religious pictures in the hallway, pink and blue saints, a Madonna in a white dress being lifted to Heaven by pretty angels, as our host led us into a room of heavy, overstuffed chairs, a big deep couch, and a long table. I wondered why there was so little light, why he didn't pull up the window shades, but this was his party and adult oddities were too many to think about one by one. Quick, jumpy, bending, smiling, his thick glasses glistening above eyes like rolling marbles, he served us the cakes on decorated plates, patting a shoulder, a head, a cheek, as he placed each dish and fork. Since I had never eaten cake with a fork, I paused, confused. But worldly Helen knew how, she had done it before, and I followed her, the smooth cut with the side of the fork, piercing the small piece, lifting it daintily to the mouth. Mr. Ricciardi didn't eat. Patting, stroking, urging more cakes and candy from a bowl on the middle of the table, he moved constantly, his fingers trembling nervously. An odd thing for someone who played the cello for a living, I thought, but maybe it was just that trembling that made the cello sound like sorrow.

While we were practicing the refined handling of unaccustomed delicacies, Mr. Ricciardi sent Helen into the next room to bring The Book. She came back with a notebook held in a rubber band. His long shaking fingers pulled at the band, and having pulled it off, he invited us to gather around him on the big sofa. As he turned the blank pages, pictures slipped from between them to lie in his lap, in ours. He was showing us something important and educational, he said. The agitated face and fingers begged us to look, to learn. Did we ever see a cock, maybe on our brothers or fathers? If not, that's what a cock was, that thing, in the bush of black hair. See the tits on that girl, they were not only for nursing babies, they were for men to squeeze and pinch. Too bad her pussy was covered with hair but we knew from our own what a pussy was like and how nice to touch. Speaking faster and faster, his fingers pointing more jumpily, he showed us naked men and women lying down close together, sometimes head to feet, like kids who had to sleep three in a narrow bed. One naked lady sat on a naked man's lap, but not on his lap exactly. I didn't really care how they arranged themselves; what horrified me were the bushes of hair. We would have them, too, Mr. Ricciardi had assured us. I didn't want it, ever, and I didn't want breasts. I wanted to stay a face, a stomach, a behind, arms and legs, no more. Helen already had two big pimples on her chest and he was stroking them while she sat there smiling plumply like Mrs. Nagy when people praised her strudel.

I didn't want anything here, not more cake, not the candy, no naked people, no bushes, no creepy, shaky hands. It was an enormous effort to get off the couch, to declare I was going, risking the accusation of being a scare-cat and spoiling the party, but I did. Helen ran after me down the hall. "You dumb stupid,

he'll give us some money soon." "I don't want it, he's scary."
"OK, you'll be sorry." Her voice changed, it wheedled. "You
won't tell my mother, will you? I'll give you some of the money
if you don't." It was a peculiar request, she knew that nobody
told on anybody about such things. Tearing a school bag, yes,
kicking in a sled, yes, stealing three cents off the newspaper stand,
yes, but not these secret happenings, never. Any crack in this
Pandora's box would open unimaginable disasters; heavy beatings
and harsh separations that would leave us truly orphaned since
we lived with one another more closely than we did with our
families. So we never betrayed one another. And our antique
wisdoms knew that it was better to appear united as a large
bouquet of flowers, fresh, innocent, untouched, and a little
stupid.

Helen's mother, Mrs. Roth, was a tall woman with the glam-
our of gray hair, which few of our mothers had. Her height and
hair gave her an authority, a dignified composure that set her
apart from the younger, frenetic mothers who argued with their
children or shouted despairingly, like Fannie Herman, at their
unheeding backs. Mrs. Roth simplified matters. When Helen was
too loud or too long in refusing to go to the grocery, Mrs. Roth
reached out her long heavy arm and slapped Helen hard, then
turned back to her ironing board and continued the flowing
hypnotic sweeps of the iron as if there had been no interruption at
all. Mrs. Roth seemed to like me. (It became a minor source of
shame in my adolescence to remember that most of the mothers
liked me because I was that abominable thing, "a good girl.")
The rare times I saw Helen's godlike brother he didn't see me at
all, although Bessie, the working sister, sometimes spoke to me.
The person I liked best in the family—my overwhelming crush on
Helen was beyond mere liking—was the bent little father. Any
time, all the time, he sat curved over a sewing machine, making

seams in pants, steadily, rapidly, working from a tall pile of cloth on a bench next to him. He was always dressed in dark shapeless pants and a worn, limp jacket, a collarless shirt buttoned up to his bony Adam's apple, and a derby, shining with age, on his head. He looked like some of the poor old widowers who hung around the synagogue, nowhere else to go, and maybe a job now and then, like dusting or sweeping the synagogue floor. He looked like some of the poor rabbis who knocked on our doors for donations to East Side yeshivas, a few pennies, a nickel. Mr. Roth was religious, otherwise why would he wear his hat indoors? The household was kosher, I knew, because Helen boasted of the four sets of dishes they had as opposed to our meager all-purpose one. Yet I never saw Mr. Roth go to the synagogue, not even on the High Holy Days when the whole contingent of Lafontaine Jews, dressed in their stiff new clothing, marched on Arthur Avenue, even my nonkosher agnostic father. (Not to go was "a shame for the *goyim*." In spite of their palpable indifference to all religions, in the main, and a tolerance that grew of immigrant interdependence, *goyim* watched and judged Jews, according to our mentor, Mr. Kaplan. Therefore, a Jew must be self-respecting in all his ways, including his religion, and show the *goyim* how unassailably upright all Jews were.) Mr. Roth had no part in this stiff-necked wariness. I never saw him outside his house; I never saw him speak to anyone but his family, and that sparsely and almost timidly.

I couldn't place Mr. Roth, who sat there, constant, in the same posture, like a statue or a piece of furniture. He couldn't be connected with people in stories or the movies. At times, when Helen was knocking around on the street, I watched him, his thin white fingers, the claws of a delicate animal, directing the cloth toward the needle, pulling back lightly, guiding again. From time to time he would talk to me over the whirr of the machine. He knew a lot of strange things, like a rabbi, though he couldn't have been one. Maybe he was some kind of special Jewish priest. (Had I been of another time and place, I might have judged him a reader of the heavens, a sorcerer.) His head bent over the machine as if it were locked in just that space, in a voice as light and delicate as his fingers, he made astonishing, terrifying revelations. When a person died, God demanded all the hair he ever had and all his fingernails. How was I ever to collect, and where, the thickets of hair that fell in the barber shop and were swept up by Tony? I would spend centuries looking through stinking piles of garbage, sewers full of rats, all over the world, for the fingernails and toenails my mother cut and threw away. I couldn't do it and God would punish me in some unimaginable way, worse than prison, worse than the electric chair. After agonized days, I asked my mother if she knew about this rule and why hadn't she warned me. She laughed and said it was Old Country superstition and not to believe everything I heard. A bit reassured, I went back to sit near Mr. Roth's machine; besides his Doomsday messages there were other pieces of arcane knowledge I might pick up, and I did. He said there were rabbis who could answer all questions, in all languages, who could make birds sing and flowers bloom, who could, themselves, fly like great eagles. He told me that numbers weren't only for school and bookkeeping; every number meant something and combinations could be powerful things. Did I know that three really meant man's heart, head, and soul working together like the notes of music? Think of seven. Did I know that there were seven planets, big earths like ours, maybe bigger? And seven days of the week. Six was holy because there were six points in the Star of David. Too bad I was a girl and not learning Hebrew, or he would show me numbers that meant more than just numbers in the Holy Books, and where, in the Books, God ordered Moses not to tell the Jews everything but leave some mysteries for other Jews to puzzle out. That was called Kabala, he said. It meant translating the letters of words into numbers and arranging them and rearranging them, and if the proper combination of letter-numbers was hit on, the great secrets of the whole world, the earth, the oceans, the stars, would be revealed and the pure soul of the discoverer could then do anything, even fly directly to God. It was more difficult to follow than long division and I couldn't imagine a soul other than as a tiny angel. That was Christian and obviously wrong. I could, a little, make letters into numbers, matching their characters: 7 was an aristocrat like capital L; 4 was squat and tough like R; 6 looked like and might be C. How to combine them, though? What secret messages to look for? I couldn't ask Mr. Roth, he might think I was trying to learn the word-number patterns he puzzled as he sewed, maybe trying to steal his answer, like copying from someone else's paper during a test. It seemed hopeless, and after hours of devising triangles, circles, and rectangles of letters and numbers, I gave it up. I sat with Mr. Roth less and less, uncomfortable because I felt I had disappointed him. Maybe he had been grooming me, a *girl* (but a Jewish girl), to become a master of Kabala. He might have seen me—among the wonderful other things floating under his old derby—as a miracle *rebbitsin*, circling the earth with the magic rabbis. Or perhaps he had assigned me the role of breathing life into huge *golems* and inspiring them to fight for the Jews. I was sorry for him and for me, but I still loved him and his frail white fingers, his curved back, his derby, and his greatest mystery: how could such a pale, shadowy spirit become the father of big, tough, clanging Helen?

12

Newer Greeners

Probably through HIAS or some organization of "landsmen"—the groupings of Old Country communities gathered for the comforts of the same dialects, for finding relatives, and for a wide variety of advice—my father dug up two antique, newly arrived immigrants who were our favorite caricatures. They were very distant relatives, but relatives nevertheless, and aged so that we had to call them Uncle Schlommke and Mimme (Aunt) Pessel, old-fashioned provincial names that enchanted my mother and, consequently, us. The Sunday visits were not frequent, but each was so superbly predictable that we children, on hearing of an impending visit, acted out every sentence of every phase. (Mimicry of neighbors, of Rosa Ponselle, of Caruso, of liturgical chant, of the iceman's Italian accent, of the janitor's Polish accent, of Mary Sugar Bum's list and wobble, was an important sport in our house.) Pessel wore a reddish wig as deeply and rigidly waved as a bronze pillar. Around her neck hung a limp fur whose beady-eyed pointed face bit its own thin tail. Under the fur, which she never removed, layers of shawls and scarves protected her delicate throat. Her long yellow face was discontented, dyspeptic; she looked as if she had a terrible taste in her mouth. Uncle Schlommke's face was round and pink cheeked; his body was round and I imagined his behind to be pink-cheeked, too. He wore a tight black derby and a long overcoat that my much taller father had given him, but when he took it off and stood in his tight suit, his belly straining the seams and buttons, he looked cute, like Tweedledee or Tweedledum.

They lived on the Lower East Side and had to take the El to visit us. Without fail Mimme Pessel arrived in a high state of agitation. A chair, please, and would someone get her a glass of water; she felt dreadful. A black man (once in a while it was an Italian) in the El had stared and stared at her and had put a curse on her, stirred up her entrails, and feel how fast her heart was beating. There was no safety from these black demons and, almost as bad, the Irishers and the "Taliener" and whoever else she could name between gasps. My mother went into the kitchen, followed by Uncle Schlommke, who liked to pat her plump arm as he examined with glistening brown eyes the food she was arranging on platters. My father, in the meantime, nodded in sympathy over Mimme Pessel while we flanked her, our heads bent like mourning angels on a Victorian tomb.

My mother carefully folded the dining room tablecloth, always with the roses tucked inside to protect them, and put on the white tablecloth on which she usually spread and stretched the immense sheet of noodle dough to be dried, then sliced with lightning speed in uncannily even slices. On the white cloth appeared the traditional Sunday night company meal: slices of salami and corned beef, a mound of rye bread, pickles sliced lengthwise, and the mild mustard the delicatessen dripped into slender paper cones from a huge bottle, gratis with each order. The drinks were celery tonic or cream soda, nectars we were allowed only on state occasions, in small glasses. Uncle Schlommke ate like a squirrel, sitting upright in his chair, his sandwich held in both hands close to his mouth, his eyes happy and searching the table as he nibbled rapidly, his red cheeks swelling, his derby rocking with each swallow. Mimme Pessel languished, sloping in her chair, one hand frequently stroking her distressed middle, and between sighs and ladylike groans made impressive amounts of meat and bread disappear, without mustard or pickle since they gave her wind. When the corned beef, of which we were given small bits because it was expensive and for company, was gone and only three or four slices of salami left and one wedge of pickle, we waited gleefully for the next development. It came from Uncle Schlommke, suddenly a wistful boy, Oliver Twist, with a thin, appealing voice. "Maybe you have a little frankfurter?" The Sunday morning shopping discussion usually included a plea for frankfurters, not only for Uncle Schlommke, who was too poor to buy them, but for us as well, who ate them almost as rarely as he. The decision was always clear and final. Frankfurters were full of unwholesome things, my father said, and he wasn't spending his money on skinsful of garbage. Uncle Schlommke's plea was given a similar answer: they were not good for the digestion and a waste of money. Embarrassed for our father and for the old man, we watched the red cheeks droop and the baby mouth pucker, appalled that he might cry, hoping he would.

It never quite happened. On the signal of the "little frankfurter," my mother began to pour tea into glasses, heaped the little cementlike cheese cakes she made on Friday and hid from us and rushed them to the table. His eyes and cheeks shone again as he stirred four lumps of sugar into his glass, tipped the tea into his saucer, and drank it in long slurps, each slurp a sigh of contentment. She was more refined, sipping more quietly out of her saucer through a lump of sugar wedged between her front teeth, "*na zukerkie*" or something like that it was called in Polish.

After tea they left, carrying a brown paper bag in which my mother had put the remaining salami and bread and cakes. We didn't think it odd that they never addressed us children, not even to ask boring questions about school or exclaim over how much we had grown. We didn't like them, we didn't dislike them; they were cartoons, displaying themselves for our amusement, like Krazy Kat. Before we realized they were people, odd, old, very poor people, they disappeared, and in the fast spinning of our worlds, we never stopped to ask why or how.

Almost everyone had newly arrived immigrants, their coming as freshening as Passover or the last day of school. The big importers were the Santinis, patiently building themselves, starting with the old settler Pete, into the Seven Brothers. Giuseppe, red-cheeked and curly haired, quickly acquired intimacy with the family truck, calling it a sonomabeech when it wouldn't start; that, and a kick, often seemed to work. He learned numbers, one-a, two-a, three-a, and got himself a girl friend from Bari who worked in the Italian market on 183rd Street. She rode with him on her time off, for love and to teach him Bronx street names. The Santinis bought another secondhand truck, a real covered moving van this time, on which we—Caroline, Petey, my brother, and I—were not permitted to play, although we still had the freedom of the first truck. It was time for another brother to arrive from Naples. Sandro wasn't as rosy and juicy-looking as Giuseppe, more long and lean like Pete, shy, and a small smiler because his teeth were rotten. One look and we didn't expect much of him and didn't get much, turning our interest to the next arrival. Mr. Kaplan had said, in one park bench conversation, that they must be paying a lot of money to get the relatives over so fast; Italians had those big family clubs that cut through "red tape"—I saw an immense red cobweb with shabby immigrants hanging on its threads like trapped flies—not like punctilious, slow-moving HIAS; the Jews always got the worst of things. We hoped the next Santini would be an actual gangster with a slanted hat, like a villain. But Ezio turned out to be big, blondish, young, a dancer and a singer who twirled us around as he sang, and he sang all the time, hopping dance songs and long-lined, sad songs that felt dark blue and lonely.

While the Santinis were filling their ramshackle attic with brothers, the Hermans were preparing for the arrival of his youngest sister, Shprinzel. She was even better than Ezio, a living replica of the "Greene Cousine." Like the Greene in the song, she didn't speak, she sang; she didn't walk, she sprang. She was as restless as Fannie, her restlessness, though, that of a bright windup toy, responsive to any touch. Everything amused her: my mother's Warsaw accent, which occasionally slipped out though she was working at tempering its broad tones; my brother's attempts to communicate with her in stumbling, no-tense Yiddish; a stove that was lit with a match set to a stinking little tube; the white and black of the piano keyboard, which she liked to slap with her big red hands to bring forth thunderous and shrill discords. She had never been to the movies, never been in a car, experiences she met first with explosive shrieks of terror and soon long hoots of joyous laughter. After a few rollicking weeks, she was given a husband, a quiet young man who worked in Mr. Herman's poultry market—no Valentino, everyone said, but steady; not "overpointed," but not really stupid, either. Fannie, like everyone else, loved Shprinzel, who was so free of her own traps of anguish and terror, and insisted that Mr. Herman spend a lot of money on his little sister's wedding. She sent her to a lady's hairdresser recommended by Mrs. Haskell, way over near the Concourse, where rich women lived, and she returned beaming between two full, thick "castle clips" on each side of her lovely, foolish face. Mr. Herman drove her down to Grand Street, where they hired a long white dress and a white veil, and to Orchard Street, where they bought a pair of black patent leather shoes, too short and pointed for her big feet. She didn't care if she had to hobble to the *chuppa*; they were beautiful, she was happy. Hobbling, burbling, waving the veil around her, chirping, laughing, down the stairs to the wedding ceremony and out of our lives. Never mind Noel Coward; "blithe spirit" means Shprinzel, her shrieks of delight and her castle clips.

We had our own two immigrants, quite unlike the radiant Shprinzel. After innumerable visits to HIAS and consultations with Workmen's Circle friends, my father arranged passage for a nephew, the grown son of one of his numerous elder sisters. My mother wasn't especially eager to welcome him; when she had suggested that one of *her* unmarried sisters be brought from Warsaw, my father had said he was spending *his* money on *his* family, not hers. She went into one of her silent, glowering times. Cousin Yankel (addressed occasionally by my father, never my mother, as Yankele, the affectionate diminutive of his name) was nineteen or twenty, lanky and awkward, with a big Adam's apple that I liked to watch riding his throat. He had a long thin nose, cheeks scored with pits and pimples, and the shortest stubble of hair on his head when he arrived. A number of immigrants arrived with shaved heads, we were told, to get rid of head lice and the trouble they might cause if immigration officials found them. Other than his Adam's apple, I liked the fact that he was double-jointed, as he demonstrated in one light moment by pushing his thumb down to touch his forearm. We thought it might be a family trait, like curly hair, and when we couldn't do

it, we felt disinherited. Yankel was bedded down on an old army
cot my father found in a Third Avenue junk store and placed
under the window in the dining-living room, an arrangement
my mother didn't like because a country cousin, a young man,
would probably not be careful of her china closet, her stone birds,
her rose-covered tablecloth, the ugly sullen rubber plant she
loved and wiped with castor oil to keep it shiningly healthy, and
he might even in his carelessness kick the piano. Clearly, she had it
in for him, and we might automatically have taken his side,
shown him some favor, if he hadn't been so indifferent to us. He
had other fish to fry. He immediately registered in a night-school
English class and was gone after supper most evenings. The remaining evenings he spent with my father to make the rounds of
acquaintances with marriageable daughters. Yankel expressed
dissatisfaction with them all; a spoiled bastard who had been
brought up in a crooning nest of women, as my father had been,
he found none of the girls pretty enough for him or, judging from
their houses and dress, rich enough. He wanted a good-looking
girl with prosperous parents, as promised him by rich America.

Of the young women he saw on the block, he mentioned a
couple of beauties. From one description we identified kitten-
faced Concetta of the family from Posilipo. She was Italian, he
was told, and the subject was immediately dismissed. The second
girl turned out to be Helen Roth's big sister, the tall laughing girl
with a shining rope of golden-brown hair who had a job in an
office downtown and often ate at the Chinks, like the rich. Was
she Jewish, maybe? Yes. Could he maybe take her for a walk after
my mother introduced them? My mother hooted vengefully.
That girl was American born, she said, a high-school graduate
who would soon be taking college night courses. She had a very
responsible, well-paying job, and who knows what high position
she might ultimately be given? She had suitors who were going to
be lawyers and doctors (we knew our mother was probably lying

but silently cheered her on as we listened) and what in the world would she want with a greenhorn? Yankel stopped mentioning local girls and went back to the search for an heiress among the landsmen. A job was an easier matter; my father was then foreman of his section in a large shoe factory and could put Yankel to work as a paid apprentice first and move him quickly to a better job.

My mother's irritation with Yankel fed and battened on his inconsiderate habits: his dirty socks on the polished piano, his night-school books pressing the breath out of the embroidered roses on her tablecloth, his habit of carefully squeezing pimples before the bathroom mirror while my brother was twisting his legs trying to hold in his pee. He wouldn't eat lung or liver, and she couldn't tell him he had to, as she did us. He ate all the farmer cheese meant for morning breakfast during his night raids on the icebox. The *klops*, a huge hamburger stewed in onion, Polish style, disappeared in one sitting, leaving nothing for the next day's lunch sandwiches. And pausing between heaping spoonfuls of *kasha*, he described the delicious things his mother, a good mother and a wonderful cook, made for him. My mother listened sourly.

There were other night raids that my mother knew nothing about. Deep in the night, Yankel would appear in his underwear at our bedroom door. He stood looking at the bed and my sister's crib for a moment, like a careful Indian scout. He came in, gently nudged my sleeping brother to the far side of our bed, nearer the wall, and waited to make sure he was still asleep. One knee on the bed, he nudged me for space. When I clung to the edge of the bed to keep him out, he stretched one long leg, and then the other, across me and settled in the middle between my brother and myself. Unlike Mr. Ricciardi, Yankel didn't care much for stroking. Fiercely whispering at me not to make any noise, he pulled off my underpants and got on top of me. He pushed his big thing, pulsating like a machine, as near as he could to my opening but never went in. Near, on top, to the side, he pressed and rose, pressed and rose, and then stayed while warm gluey stuff spilled down my thighs. He got up, said nothing, and tiptoed down the hall to his dining room cot. Once, when a noise came from the baby's crib, he ran on tiptoe to the bathroom to make it appear, I suppose, that he had just gotten up to pee.

After several nights of this—I can't remember how or if they were spaced—I decided that this was bad and dangerous. There were adult phrases around the street and on park benches about the girl who died because Fatty Arbuckle had torn her. I seemed also in danger of being torn. When my brother and sister were fast asleep, I took the extra blanket hanging over the end of the bed, wrapped myself in it, and sat down in the chair on which we had draped our clothing, determined to spend that night, and all others if necessary, sitting up. He came in, stared, groped in the bed, and turned to find me sitting. He began to plead with me to go back to bed. He wouldn't touch me, never again. What would my mother think if she found me that way? Please go back to bed. Please don't say anything. He could be arrested and sent back to Poland if I said anything. He'd give me a beautiful present, a gold ring, if I went back to bed. Please. Please. I stared at him and said nothing. He looked at me out of his pimpled face for a while—waiting for what?—and then tiptoed down the hall.

Since my mother didn't like him and my brother was totally indifferent to him, the fact that I stopped talking to him at all made no conspicuous change in our lives. Not too long after I felt it safe to sleep in my bed again he said he had found a man from his province with whom he was going to share a room as a boarder, nearer the factory. I knew he was lying but only stared at him as insolently as Helen Roth did at her Italian cellist neighbor. The next day, when I came home from school, he was gone and my mother was practicing her mandolin in her dining room, with the red tablecloth roses fluffed, the birds pecking in their white stone bowl, the rubber plant gleaming with castor oil.

Our next greenhorn was my father's niece, Beile, another sister's child, an even more avid go-getter than skinny Yankel and his spills of semen. She insisted, after her first week in night school, that her name was Beth and kept on insisting until my father told her it was a Christian name and Bessie would be better. Bessie it was. She was older than Yankel, in her mid-twenties, and, as the neighbors said, no "greene." She was already remarkably sharpened for survival. It didn't matter to her that my brother and I needed a child's full sleep; since she shared our bed, she had a right to keep us awake to hear her lessons in grammar and spelling. At first I didn't mind. She was novel, she learned fast, she had hair like mine, a thatch of all flaxen and blond colors. And I could play teacher without contradictions or fights. My brother slept through most of those long, thorough lessons as she went over and over each word until she made not one mistake. I began to hate her but said nothing until my mother asked me why I was dragging myself around like a sleepwalker. When I told her about Bessie's keeping me awake to study with her, she had a short discussion with my father behind closed doors and it stopped.

Not altogether. Bessie decided I was good for other things besides spelling. I would wake up during the night to find her legs tightly wrapped around my thigh as she rubbed herself against it with mounting vigor and speed, moaning little sighs of pleasure and shaking; stopping and starting again. She was as greedy for pleasure as for learning English. Of course I knew what she was doing, but I had never known it to be on someone else's thigh; a pillow, a towel, a hand, but a thigh? Maybe that was the way they did it in Poland and I wondered who her partners had been.

This didn't happen too frequently, nor did it last very long, and since I always made believe I was asleep and felt more curious than menaced, I didn't worry about it. Although my brother was a dedicated sleeper—each night a hibernation rather than the drop and lift of the shallow river of sleep in which I swam—he must have been occasionally aware of what went on in his bed with Yankel, with Bessie. He never mentioned it; he knew the code. Don't tell on anyone, don't rock any boats; save the troubles for something with fairly predictable results, like nagging for a bicycle or going on the rides in Coney Island.

There were advantages to having Bessie around; she now went on those long evening walks with my father, much more eager than I had ever been. They were dreaming a business career for her, I suspected. I heard many years later that she made a lot of money for herself and some for my father, too. He took her, as he had Yankel, on a round of visits among Workmen's Circle friends, among union mates, again with matrimony in mind. She may have then been his mistress (almost certainly later), but it was important to have her married. No raving beauty, she wore glasses, weak-eyed like several in my father's family. She was blond, blue-eyed, and spirited, though, and eager to follow whatever Uncle told her she must do. He found her a husband quickly, a fellow worker named Moe, who was small and thin with soft flat brown hair and glasses. (When they kissed, would their glasses clash?) He rarely said anything when he came to the house, always appearing with a Whitman's Sampler box of chocolates for her and a couple of Baby Ruths for us. Then he sat, drinking tea, for which he thanked my mother in a low voice, listening to Bessie, listening to my father, awed by the speed and number of their words. We didn't have to be polite with Moe and hang around as if he were company; we could disappear with our candy and no one cared.

When it was established that they were engaged (my mother said, and she might have been right or just enjoying herself, that my father took Moe to a jeweler of his acquaintance on Canal Street, himself picked out the engagement ring, and himself bargained the price down while Moe stood silently by), my father became their duenna, accompanying them to the movies and the Chinks on Tremont Avenue and visits to distant cousins. The evenings without them were lovely gifts. We could talk and even fight lightly; our mother taught us to dance the mazurka and the krakowiak, and she sang to her mandolin. We dressed up our little sister as "Sandy Claws" by tying pillows and a red cloth around her; we made her one of the Seven Dwarfs with an absorbent cotton beard; we made her a bride with one of the curtains my mother had just washed. She was still afraid of our size and noise, examining us guardedly with her big golden eyes, but, invited to shelter on our mother's lap during intermissions she slowly came around, trying to dance and sing with us. We were happy enough, my brother and I, to tell her how well she danced and sang, and she did, considering that she was all eyes, fat baby legs, and fat baby belly. Once in a while I had one fleeting regret: that I wasn't out with Moe, Bessie, and my father at the Chinks. It certainly wasn't their company I missed. I wanted to pour brown-red sauce made of Chinamen's blood on pork ribs, which I had never tasted, and maybe I would drop dead and get into all the papers. And I hoped to find a Chinese pinkie, chopped off by a sword, among the pieces of Chinese chicken. When I once mentioned ruefully to my mother that I wished they had taken me to the Chinks, she dismissed me, once again, as one of those creatures who wanted to dance at all weddings; nosy, restless, discontented.

It took a long, exasperating time for Bessie to marry her Moe. In the meantime, she got a job in a corset factory and babbled

English shockingly well, making few of the mistakes my mother did. In the English classes at the public library they apparently made an unforgettable point of the fact that a plural noun was signaled by a final "s": "girl, girls," "pot, pots." Thereafter, until the day of her death, and after the acquisition of polished written Yiddish, decent English, perfect Polish, and fluent conversational Italian, my mother avoided "lettuce" for one head, pronouncing it, carefully, "lettu," a chic Frenchy sound, we thought; the icebox was always the "icebock." We enjoyed "lettu" and "icebock" too much to correct her, something we were ordinarily not reluctant to do.

Back to the golden girl, Bessie. My father began to bring home samples, exquisite handmade shoes, in size four and a half, narrow, Cinderella shoes my mother couldn't wear; she was a wide six. They fit Bessie, always showing off her dainty feet and hands, and I looked on in misery as she pranced around in silky suede carved in tiny flowers on graceful heels. There was some conversation behind the closed bedroom door, and shortly after, my father brought home two pairs, one for me. They fit tightly but they fit, the color and smoothness of a faun, a rosette of suede at the instep. I was beside myself and even kissed him in thanks. Another conversation behind closed doors the next day. My father emerged to say that he had made a mistake, those shoes should not have been taken out of the factory, but he would buy me another pair, soon. I knew what kind they would be: strong, well made, good for school, and flat-heeled. Worse still, we would have to go through *that* conversation with the salesman once again: my father expansively the expert sample-maker, the salesman listening respectfully, his silly head to one side, an admiring little smile on his face. It was going to be deeply embarrassing, trying not to listen, staring down at my shoeless, vulnerable feet. After time had stopped dead still, the choice would be made, not mine, but the pair with thick shit-colored laces, then the blood-covered money paid out. Mourning at my assiduously accumulated graveyard mound of broken promises and disappointments, I retreated into my tower of silence. We'll buy shoes after the movies on Saturday. I shook my head, no. You need shoes. No. Denying them access to the usual weapons, I practiced the piano seriously, a whole half-hour for scales, each piece meticulously allotted its time so my father of the hundred ears wouldn't call out, "What about that new nocturne, the one for the recital?" The baby was walked around and around the block for her full dose of fresh air, and I didn't forget to buy the gluey farina on our way home. My mother couldn't say "Where's your head?" or warn that I was growing up to be a "*luftmensh*," a floater on clouds. That silence was a powerful place: my brother kept out of my way, my mother's face looked as if it were shut in a dark closet; my father yelled, once again, that my mother was breeding a white silent snake and slammed the door as he went out in his new hat and coat to a Workmen's Circle meeting.

It is curious that though I remember the Hermans' Shprinzel so vividly and happily as a bride, I cannot remember Bessie's marriage and departure at all; obviously I was glad to have her erased. The rare times that Yankel and Bessie come to mind, they appear with a chapter title: "The Wet Seasons," the steamy jungle time of semen and coiling female moistures; the rest, the shrewd intelligence, the variety of greeds and ambitions, remain as thin abstractions. That Bessie was, finally, married came at us tangentially. My father's outings diminished, he was around more. We heard by the usual eavesdropping on the kitchen conversations during homework time in the dining room that the "*chommer*" (dope) Moe frequently complained about Bessie during the factory lunch break. She spent his money faster than he could earn it; she didn't want to buy on Orchard or Division Street but found her way to the uptown stores, not even afraid of Altman's on

Fifth Avenue. Fifth Avenue, mind you. She didn't want to stop working and have children—he loved children—not at least until he helped her buy a corset shop. When he came home tired from the factory, she slapped any old thing on the table and told him to eat fast, they were going to the movies or Maurice Schwartz's theater on Second Avenue, hurry up, for God's sake. Sometimes she didn't come home until nine or ten, working overtime, while he ate a roll and butter for supper; there was nothing in the icebox. My father laughed and my mother laughed. They were disgusting; what had skinny little Moe ever done to them that they should laugh like spiders watching a fly struggle in their web? True, my mother hadn't enmeshed Moe—my father had— but to be so indifferent, so amused, so un-noble, so unlike the gentle, generous women in books; she was truly disgusting.

Still cocooned in my silences, I practiced demonically for the borough piano contest, the same contest in which I had won a bronze medal the year before. Every kind of nervousness assailed me as I prepared. I anticipated falling on the stage steps, wrong notes in pieces I knew perfectly well, my foot frozen on the pedal, making howling noises when I should be tapping gently, my bowels churning and running as they did with Friday morning arithmetic tests. As I walked up the stairs of the school auditorium toward the piano, I did what I had to for getting through and surviving. The frightened, trembling, bellyached person was pushed far away. The other person, bowing, sitting, striking the notes, and pushing the pedals, was cool, indifferent. It didn't matter if she forgot a passage or her fingers jumbled in a fast run, or she slipped off the piano bench or dirtied her pants; all that might happen in the distant place of the scared, shaking one and had nothing to do with here.

It went well, silver-medal well, and I went home carrying my medal with a harp on one side and stately words on the other in

my wet, quivering hand. The school had also presented me with a
small bouquet, of which I remember only the tremulous baby's
breath that seemed to be tiny people echoing my excitement as I
strode through the dark streets ahead of my family and a few
neighbors. We had store-bought fancy cake and were allowed to
stay up extra-late even for a Friday night. Too excited, too tired,
worried whether this triumph would revive my father's dream of
me as a concert pianist, I couldn't talk much, but the icy silence
had to begin melting.

13

Brothers and Fathers

My brother stamped and twisted as my mother tried to tie a woolen scarf around his neck, making him look like a sissy, he growled. "Sissy" was the worst a boy could be, a boy who now went to school and adventured only with a knights' circle that severely abjured females according to holy rules. Never touch a girl's library book no matter how attractive its pictures; hiss "Mush" in concert when the Sheik folds his pale captive in his warrior-banded arms and beams his dark eyes on her trembling mouth; never listen to an older sister but always report her street iniquities; refer to a younger sister as "that dopey kid." Interfering with the idiotic female pleasures of bouncing balls and jumping ropes was a constant duty of the knighthood, as triumphant an accomplishment as finding the Holy Grail. Their Camelot was a thicket on the Monterey lot, their sacred festival something they spoke of in whispers as "King of the Hill." (It was called "House on Fire" on less romantic streets.) This mysterious ritual held us girls in awe; we tried to spy but guards ran us away, the more dedicated with handfuls of pebbles and sticks. Before these holy rites took place the boys baked stolen potatoes, "mickies" (after the Irish word for potato, "mick") lifted from grocery bins and green stores while the proprietor was busy elsewhere, although the men probably knew what was happening. One's own kid might at this very moment be robbing a competitor, and one potato, what the hell; there was a rough justice in the arrangement and the boys sensed it. Lifting a mickie was playing at stealing, while swiping a couple of nigger babies from the candy store was real theft and thrillingly fearsome with potential for beatings and arrest by the implacable blue mountains of cops. (The girls, trying for masculine freedoms, did a little of this stealing, as well. I tried it twice, one nickel and four pennies off a newsstand, a yellow pencil from the five-and-ten, and then gave it up because I suffered inordinately. Some book said that the eyes were the windows of the soul, whatever important thing that was, and I couldn't raise them to my mother or teacher, who would see through my eyes the black stain on my soul. I was accused and punished by every unexpected sound, by every small misfortune like breaking a dish, by a mistake in arithmetic. I walked for days in stomach pain and black mists and thus became a reasonably honest person.)

After the feasting on burnt mickies—on an exchange deal I made with my brother, he brought me a cold piece, ashes outside, raw inside, and inedible—at their Round Table, the "King of the Hill" ritual took place in their lot chapel. One afternoon Minnie Rosen and I went up to her roof, in the middle of the block, and looking down, saw an astonishing, disappointing, profoundly enlightening sight. The mickie fire was being fed more sticks and twigs, and when it reached a high, bright magnificence, the boys unbuttoned their pants and put the fire out with their piss. And that was it. It was always fun to catch a glimpse of a boy's thing if one could, and here there were eight or ten, more to be imagined than seen at that distance, but unmistakably there and streaming in those enviable arches. Minnie, the toy and victim of older brothers who cuffed her and bought her candy, and a cynic, said, "I could have told you it was nothing, just a dumb game." My responses were more complicated; the first impulse was to run to my mother to tell her about the dirty thing my brother was doing. I didn't. My brother had just been beaten after yet another graphic, detailed description of the rats, the bread and water in the airless, lightless solitude of the prison that would enfold his life, and while he was shouting and peeing like a happy savage around the fire, I still stung from his terror and pain. Something else was happening, too, a letdown I had to think about, a different view of the male world. I felt as I walked down from the roof that their secrets were not so impenetrable or even worth penetrating. If it was a "man's world," as the women kept saying, it wasn't all that remarkable. The actuality of the "King of the Hill," the masterful name for a feeble power that was an accident of birth—being able to pee standing up—was my first primitive experience of feminism, enhanced by my father's irrational furies and my brother's wails. I might try myself against that world of paper strengths.

The experiment of a jump from the highest rock, a sheer tall cliff in Crotona Park, exclusively the terrain of boys, had mixed but unexpectedly rewarding results. I was afraid to jump and, as usual, more afraid not to, and I slipped off the edge, to land cross-kneed and incapable of getting up. There must have been pain but I remember only the incredulous fact of my legs being useless, as my brother's had been long ago. Some sort of vengeance? I believed in vengeance as a world force, like the sun rising every day and the change of seasons. Somewhere there was a vast hall, an auditorium where there were scrolls of happenings that had to be paid for, sins waiting for the "Vengeance of God," who kept careful records like truant officers.

By falling rather than jumping, I lost my chance to be a "tomboy" semirespected by the real boys. Instead I entered a time of joyous queenliness. The baby was taken out of her go-cart and given to my father to carry, and I put into it, my mother, finally, finally, pushing *me* in a carriage while my brother, who also enjoyed all irregular situations, pushed along with her. On the way out of the park, the benches full of Sunday grown-ups, the girls making buttercup chains, the boys skimming rocks in the pond, the babies crawling in the grass, everyone asked, "What happened?" and were told in full, lingering detail as they stared at *me*. The gardeners scraping the flower beds asked what happened, and Mrs. Katz came out of her candy store to be told, holding a hand to her cheek, shaking her head in worried disbelief. Some of the kids hanging around the store followed my carriage. It was a progress worthy of Elizabeth I, leisured and regal, which continued through most of that Sunday afternoon. As we neared our house, my mother ran across to the De Santis garage, and the eldest boy, Federico, one of the beloved incandescences too beautiful to look at, came back with her and carried me in his arms, like Agnes Ayres, to his car and drove me to Fordham Hospital. Some slight disappointment there: no thick casts, no steel braces, no surgical armor of leather and straps as I had seen in the Sunday *American*; no pathos of crutches, not even bandages. The doctor said I was to stay in bed for a week. He insulted me, so special and frail, by saying I was a healthy youngster and a week in bed would fix my pulled muscles fine. Federico carried me out to the car and drove us home, and my father carried me up the five flights of stairs as he had done when I was a very little girl and fell asleep among the coats on Uncle David's bed when we went there for Passover.

The week was a dream of omnipotence. My food was brought to me in bed, and extra Lorna Doones and Fig Newtons with my afternoon milk. The baby's crib was taken out of our room and put into our parents' bedroom. My brother slept on two chairs in the living room to avoid kicking my delicate legs. He was told he might play with me but any rough stuff and he would be banished from my royal presence. Ruthie and Minnie came every afternoon to bring me my homework assignments and a note printed—like a book—with GET WELL SOON from our teacher, Miss Monahan. I greeted them languidly, spoke to them in a thin voice, asked them please not to shake the bed, and generally, as my mother began to complain after a few days, acted like a *kimpeturen*, a woman in childbed to whom these languors rightfully belonged. Like all halcyon glories, this, too, waned, and after a brief rekindling of interest when I returned to school, vanished altogether.

The trials of strength weren't over, though. Walking with my eyes shut, feeling my way along the walls and furniture, tried me in the world of the blind. Limping lightly or deeply, hobbling, sliding, twisting my feet far inward, walking on one ankle, proved I could be a successful cripple. Holding my hands over my ears made a silence that was insupportable; I couldn't make it in the world of the deaf. When my mother caught me playing blind or crippled, she was, I thought, excessively disturbed. She said I was odd, peculiar (a stamp as indelible as a concentration camp number), and ordered me to stop being Susie Bren (Burn), a caricature of a fiery actress. If my father caught me, he said I was crazy, and then she leaped, she thought, to my defense, countering once again with my resemblance to *his* sister, the one who had died in a madhouse. A plague on both their houses; I'd show them not how odd but how distinguished I was and as accomplished as any boy. In our repertoire of heroes were the older boys on skates who grabbed at the backs of passing trucks and, holding on to a chain, a rope, anything, flew with them as far as Southern Boulevard, as far as the Grand Concourse, as far as West Farms. It was dangerous, a sudden stop or turn might throw a boy hard enough to break his head or smash him under the wheels of another car. And absolutely forbidden, the repeated prohibition embroidered with horror stories of the Irish boy from Arthur Avenue whose neck was broken and who would probably be paralyzed all his life; the Italian boy on Third Avenue who died, a bundle of broken bones, in Fordham Hospital. There were no Jewish boys among the examples; they were too obedient to play such suicidal games was the implication. As eager to try the big boys' world as I, my brother joined me in hitching on the backs of trucks, an important act of complicity that required a coordination of lies. We still informed on each other, we still fought—often in itself an act of complicity, designed to annoy *them*—but we had honed fine the antennae that sensed out the times for mutual protection. We were both fast, skillful skaters, and although our few breathless words during these flights were my powerful, motherly "Hold on tight" and his "Shut up," some respect for each other's capacities moved subtly, always mutely, between us. I found myself thinking, He's only a little boy, for God's sake—as he might have been thinking, She's only a girl, for God's sake.

His opportunities were much greater than mine. After six months of practice that ruined the kitchen clock, which he kept on the piano to push ahead so that his practice hour might be completed in twenty minutes, my parents decided his lessons were a waste of money. I continued to practice, never betraying that I sometimes enjoyed it; a stream of grumbling and sullen lurching was the required way to approach practice. His role with our baby was to kootchy-koo her as he dashed in from school and down to the street while I thumped the carriage down the five flights, up and down again with the pillows and blankets, up and down again with the baby. While he, the grasshopper, sang and danced, I, the ant, sat demurely rocking the carriage. He was in the full sun, I in shade; he was young, I was old. When I caught sight of him hitching on a truck on one of the cross streets—never on our informer block—my fury was fire in my limbs. By telling my mother the baby had coughed and sneezed a lot on the street, she was surely getting a cold; by swearing I had sprained my hand in school and couldn't possibly practice, I made time to latch on to trucks, too. Often, finding the sky darkening and the street names altogether unfamiliar—Prospect, Intervale, Westchester, Burnside—I pulled us both away and started the journey home, slipping again into the irresistible role, burdensome and magnificent, of telling him not to worry, I knew our way home. I did know it, having observed the outward journey, a deeply embedded habit planted in many places, now rooted in Crotona Park, where lingering over a bright insect in the grass, or splashing in a puddle, or picking up a dusty lost marble evoked from my father the "teach him a lesson" act. He would push us all behind a big tree, to watch my brother suddenly look around, his face half-speaking, breaking into bewilderment, then tears. Sometimes my mother ran back to him; usually it was I.

It was at about this time of strengthening to disobedience and daring that a chivalric battle took place at Lafontaine, in front of the hat factory. It was a warm spring afternoon and five or six of us were playing potsy on the broader sidewalk there; no interfering house stoops and the ugly humpbacked watchman had not yet arrived to yell at us for chalking up his street ("I brek you henk 'n feet ven I see you"). Suddenly, from Arthur Avenue, a gang of boys, big boys, came loping down 179th Street and surrounded us. Taunting, foulmouthed, saying things we didn't understand but knew were dirty, they began to lift our skirts and poke at our chests. Hearing the yells of "Get-outa-here" and "Maaa," a group of boys sprawled over a game of marbles down the street leaped up and some of them began to run toward us; the rest remained fixed on the marbles, afraid of this formidable gang. One of the few who came running was my brother, who jumped at the boy trying to grope under my skirt and began to tear at him, trying to pull his arm away. The tall gang boy shouted, "I'll shoot your sister full of scum, shrimpy," and met a small, whirling fury, pummeling, scratching, kicking. A couple of men, coming out of the factory for a smoke, sent Arthur Avenue about its business with a show of clenched fists. My brother's shirt was torn and his lip swelling, but he sauntered back to the marbles game as cool and expressionless as Elmo Lincoln. That night I was, as usual, blamed for the shirt and the lip. Instead of battling the injustice of my situation, as was expected, I explained that he got into a fight with an Arthur Avenue boy who was bothering me. He said, "Yeah." My mother asked what the boy had done, and I said, "Oh, nothing. He was just pushing and trying to make me fall while I was playing potsy." I knew what she really wanted to know, whether my skirt was lifted and my place touched. I wasn't about to tell her; as long as she kept her secrets, I would keep mine. I wished I had the nerve to ask my brother exactly what "shooting full of scum" meant; it wasn't fair that he knew things I didn't. Still, as often in such vague and momentous matters, I knew enough to put the phrase in its proper category, dim and wide as that was: the place of shut bedroom doors, of people squirming on hot roofs, of dogs stuck together, of how babies were seeded or peed or stuffed into bellies.

Of course I never thanked my brother or praised him, but I must have been impressed, and in spite of my parents' infuriatingly boring injunctions that I take care of him, watch him, don't let him get dirty, and, and, and, and, I began to release him more and more to himself. Furthermore, I had become chummy with some older girls who *knew everything*. I intended to concentrate on "shooting scum" and related matters with them and was determined to brook no distractions. We ten- and eleven-year-olds hinted and giggled at each other over key words: "things," "breasts," "love," but we were still lost, though we tried for slant-eyed looks of wisdom, like Anna May Wong.

One of the older girls, twelve, was new on the block. Her name was Deborah May, but she liked to be called Debby, like one of the blond paper dolls she claimed to scorn, baby stuff. She said her mother had a permanent that cost five dollars and a lipstick that she let Debby use sometimes. We younger girls granted her wonder and admiration as we recognized our own lies. No use in accusing her of lying, of antagonizing her. She had things to tell us, and for that, we could accept her garbage. She was the teacher of menstruation, the "monthlies" that all women got and had to use rags for. Each month, Debby informed us, the thighs separate from the lower belly, held only by a thin thread of skin. From these immense gashes, which I saw as the deep wide cuts made by a butcher's cleaver as he severed a leg from the rest of carcass, flowed blood, rivers of blood, for days and days. She told it coolly, clinically, but it disturbed my sleep for days and weeks; the thighs hanging by a skin thread appeared on my geography page, the twin rivers of blood on the sheets of the Mozart sonata I was practicing. Alternating with my periods of crippled limping and stumbling blindness, I tried to walk as if I had a mound of bloody rags between my legs. How come I never saw a woman walk that way? I thought that Debby might be wrong on another score, too—anyone so hideously butchered must surely die after one monthly—but I had to trust her because she knew and told, which no one else would. (Her nightmare picture remained so convincingly vivid that when I actually began to menstruate and found some drops of blood on my bloomers I had no idea of what was happening, made no connection with Debby's enlightenments.)

The next set of lessons, by big, bosomy Italian Rosa, left with the Bianchis while her parents went back to Caltanisetta to find a bride for her eldest brother, was less gloom, more fun and variety. Her specialty was the most important one, "shooting scum," who does it, how it's done, and other unbelievable things, including the fact that scum makes babies. Her approach was juicily conspiratorial. She would teach only on the foreign territory of Monterey, her pupils a select few sworn to secrecy: big Helen, who knew a lot about bushy hair from the pictures in her neighbor's house but needed filling in on other details; Ruthie Meilman, with lank brown hair and a sharp little nose like a mouse, a showoff who liked to masturbate on a pillow near her kitchen window so everyone in the courtyard could see; Minnie Rosen, who stammered; by courtesy, Carlotta Bianchi, Rosa's cousin and really too dumb to care; and myself. Rosa was a good teacher, a skilled raconteur who supplied specific identities, a cousin, an uncle, an aunt, to make her lessons vivid, immediate. Apparently she spent a good deal of her time prowling, peeping into keyholes or gaps in warped doors. (She was too graphic to be only a voyeur, we suspected, she must have been a participant too; all the better, more real.) First, the vocabulary lesson. A man's thing was a prick or a cock, a woman's hole a twat. If a lady stroked a man's prick, it would become big and fat and he would ram it in her twat and keep ramming until they both had a shivering pain that made them yell and then they stopped. Sometimes the lady rode the man's thing like a horse until the shivering came and she fell on him. Sometimes he turned her over, pulled her ass up, and rode her like a big dog until he shook and collapsed. Afterward they looked sweaty and the bed smelled of the man's scum. And there was apocrypha too difficult to believe, about pinching and slapping and tasting and sucking, and a story about her uncle Sandro who got stuck inside her aunt Assunta; they had to be pulled apart by her uncles Tullio and Gino. I didn't think the story was funny, people stuck like dogs, and some of the rest was beyond acceptance, but accept it I must have, since I fought it all so bitterly. The swelling and pushing, the sweating like the hot shine of the butcher shop, the smell like singed chickens, the contortions like the roof people—that's not how I was born or our cute baby who blew milk bubbles. This couldn't be what they meant by "So they lived happily ever after" when Cinderella and the Prince got married, when Beauty married the beautiful Beast, when Assunta Paterno in a long white veil kissed Sandro Bondi in their church, all this crazy stuff mixed up with places for peeing and shitting. No and no and no.

The lighter contributions Rosa brought from Carmine Street were much more acceptable. In our long ball-bouncing and rope-jumping careers, we had progressed from the limpid dopiness of

> *One, two, three a-lairy (right leg over ball in midair)*
> *I spy Mrs. Sairy (leg over)*
> *Sitting on a Bumbleairy (ditto)*
> *Just like a chocolate fairy (ditto)*

and

> *Teddy Bear, Teddy Bear, turn around*
> *Teddy Bear, Teddy Bear, touch the ground*
> *Teddy Bear, Teddy Bear, show your shoe*
> *Teddy Bear, Teddy Bear, please skiddoo*
> *Teddy Bear, Teddy Bear, go upstairs*
> *Teddy Bear, Teddy Bear, say your prayers*

to chants that recognized school life, family life, marriage, careers, and death:

> *Ding, dong, ding, dong, ding, dick*
> *Here comes the teacher with the big fat stick*

Now get ready for arithmetic
One and one are two
Two and two are four
Now get ready for spelling—
C-a-t, cat; r-a-t, rat

Bouncy, bouncy, ballee
I let the baby fallee
My mother came out
And slapped my mouth
Bouncy, bouncy, ballee

Johnny on the ocean, Johnny on the sea
Johnny broke the sugar bowl
And blamed it all on me
I told Ma, Ma told Pa
Johnny got a licking
Ha! Ha! Ha!

A long-lasting chant, a specialty of practiced jumpers, was a trip through the alphabet:

A, my name is Alice
My husband's name is Al
We live in Albany
And we sell apples.

B, my name is Bessie
And my husband's name is Ben
We live in Boston
And we sell balloons.

And so on.

Several songs ended in rapid counting when both rope and jumper took on a frantic pace:

> Fudge, fudge, tell the Judge
> Mama's got a baby
> Not a boy, not a girl
> Just a little lady
> Wrap her up in tissue paper
> Send her to the elevator
> How many pounds does she weigh?
> Ten, twenty, thirty, forty, fifty, etc.

> Mother, mother, I am sick
> Send for the doctor quick, quick, quick
> Doctor, doctor, will I die
> Yes, my daughter, by and by
> How many hours will it take?
> Ten, twenty, thirty, forty—

Rosa added new spice to our games with:

> My sister had a baby, his name was Sonny Jim
> She put him in a pisspot, to teach him how to swim
> He swam to the bottom, he swam to the top
> My sister got excited and pulled him by the—

Uncontrollable giggling here. I liked better the piquant imagery of:

> Old Mr. Kelly had a pimple on his belly
> His wife bit it off and it tasted like jelly.

We didn't have the essential meaning of this one but the salacious aura was pleasurably there.

After the active grapevine of Lafontaine mothers and brothers
had delivered some lurid details, we were forbidden to talk with
Debby and Rosa. Their remembered voices, their excited faces,
their troubling information helped make a rocky voyage of my
eleventh to twelfth year.

I fought more with my disgusting mother and braved louder
disobedience to my disgusting father, and while I fought, I tried
to shape the breasts under her housedress and pierce the front
buttons of his pants. As I walked to school, to the movies, to the
library, I looked for the shape of breasts—titties, Rosa had called
them—and "things," not yet ready for "prick." I began to examine myself carefully, to search my armpits for hairs and my breasts
for signs of swelling. My friends were proud to report a body hair
or two and boasted of soon needing "bassiers." I tore out the hairs
I found in my armpits with my fingernails. When my breasts
began to swell with horrifying rapidity, I searched the sewing
machine drawers for cloths and ribbons to tie around them, to
stop them. My mother had brought from Warsaw wide pink and
blue silk ribbons that she had used in her shop and, when I let her,
had put in my hair. I lifted one of these, a blue one, out of the
machine and took it to the bathroom, undressed, and tied it
tight, tight, around my chest, and dressed again. The ribbon was
never tight enough, never stopped the ghastly swelling. I pulled it
tighter and still tighter until it dug long cuts under my arms, the
blood staining the ribbon. Still I pulled. Still I swelled.

My mother never saw the cuts or the bloodied ribbon; by now
I was insisting on, shrieking for, intense privacy during the
weekly bath, and on dressing and undressing in the bathroom
instead of the room I shared with my brother and the baby. The
baby didn't matter, but my normally sleepy, indifferent brother
might just open his eyes at the wrong time, look, and ruin my life
once again by commenting on my cuts in his clear choirboy voice.

My mother would ask questions, scold me for the scars that might give me blood poison and for the dirty, dried-blood ribbon, once so lovely, all the way from Warsaw. There were other matters involved, dimly reasoned, strongly felt. The ribbons were another test of strength, of stoicism, and a denial of sexuality, of being filthily conceived, the need for privacy an evolutionary step in the gathering of myself as me, solely me, a separation from the strangling claustrophobia of four people continuing too long to be one.

If I didn't want to talk, I wouldn't. I was good in school, except in arithmetic, could play Chopin's "Fantasie Impromptu" fast with all the notes clear and the slow part sweet, sad, and deep; under my care the baby carriage turned over only once, the baby unhurt, smiling as she slid out with her pillows; my brother hadn't been run over while I jumped rope, a standard prophecy. Miss Torrence let me walk a few blocks with her after school, asking me what I thought about "Chickie" in the Sunday *American*, and I answered freely and wisely. After we had a geography lesson on Italy and I wrote a composition about Venice, she asked me when I had been there, it sounded as if I had. Miss Califano, who let me erase the blackboard once, said I was pretty. My skin still crawled with shame when I remembered stupid things I had said, cruel things I had done, lies I had told, but I could no longer be convinced—in spite of my father—that I was the worst girl in the world and the ugliest. For his own interesting reasons, my father called me "Luna Park" when I smiled, the reference to the huge-mouthed, moon-faced advertisement for the Coney Island amusement park. I stopped smiling or tried to, tying my face into a grotesque knot to show only my top front teeth. Whereupon my brother said I looked like a big rabbit, so I had to practice making my mouth smaller, biting my upper lip while I tightened the lower, pouting like Mae Murray, studying the shapes other people's mouths made and imitating them as I lay in bed before I fell asleep. But I was not the ugliest girl in the world.

At the corner grocery where I went for prunes, a constant of our icebox that my father considered a major lifeline to health, and that we (in the innumerable little acts of feeble vengeance that were *our* lifeline) never ate, I found the usual gaggle of women talking with more than their usual animation, their voices hopping over one another. They were discussing a contest announced by a Jewish newspaper, soliciting pictures of candidates for the prettiest Jewish girl in New York. She would be named Queen Esther, get gorgeous presents, be given a big party by the editors, and have her picture printed in the paper. Two of the women turned to me and said, "Why doesn't your mother send *your* picture in? Mrs. Halpern is sending in her Miriam and Mrs. Katz her Hannah. You're prettier, much prettier than they." I didn't say anything and didn't know what to do with my face; to smile would appear show-offy, not to smile was to be "*mudne*" (odd). I ran out of the store stuffed with rainbows, down the street and up the stairs to our apartment, calling "Ma!" as I pushed the door open, shouting as I ran down the hallway asking if she knew about the Queen Esther contest and wouldn't she send my picture in. She knew about it and wouldn't send my picture in. I was too young, you had to be at least thirteen, and anyhow my father would never permit it. But I was big enough to pass for thirteen—people often said that—and wouldn't she please, please, try to persuade my father. She shrugged doubtfully and sent me back to get the prunes for which the water was already boiling.

That night nothing was said at supper and nothing afterward while I did my homework and listened. Nothing. My mother read a letter from Warsaw of which I now understood only the salutation, something like "kochana shustra," Dear Sister, and then she boiled the diapers while he read the paper. The next night and the next, nothing. I was as good as gold, practiced and practiced and didn't slam doors. It wasn't possible though, it never was, for me to sit with the rest at Sunday breakfast in spite of the big fresh rolls and farmer cheese on the table. On Sunday mornings there lay on the table a fatty *matjes* herring with oily accusing eyes and an oily, dead tail. It was left to my father's enthusiastic connoisseurship, as lively and contentious as I later found in martini connoisseurs, to make the purchase in the delicatessen on 178th Street, the only food purchase he ever made. Come flu epidemics, teething, postabortion pains, chicken pox, mumps, measles, a man should never carry grocery packages. How could he carry this one, a monstrosity in stinking, fat-stained Jewish newspaper that made me want to vomit? It was after several struggles during which I sat heaving, threatening to vomit, that I was permitted to have Sunday breakfast, corn flakes and milk, very early and alone, another concession to my oddness. That special Sunday, inspired by the vision of myself in the long golden dress and jeweled crown of Queen Esther, I made restitution for not sitting with them and the herring by drawing a picture of the baby's profile, a little fruit bowl of curves and pouts. They liked it, even my brother. This might be the right climate for asking about the contest, and I did, choosing my words carefully, not allowing the spill of enthusiasm that would result in the absolute final dismissal of "Nonsense! Don't be crazy." My mother said nothing, the stage was my father's. I was too young, that was for sure, he said, and didn't I know that beauty contest winners didn't become movie actresses, as I hoped to become, but street girls, too spoiled to go to school to learn typing and stenography and become secretaries for good salaries? We were, I knew, approaching white slavery gangs and the vicious brothels of Buenos Aires and my bitterness was threatening to become visible tears. He mustn't think he could make me cry. I ran to my refuge, the locked bathroom, where I stood and held myself together, literally, as if my bones had been broken and I must knit them up again.

When I came out, my mother asked if I didn't want to take the picture of the baby to school to show my teacher, it was very nice. No, she could do with it as she liked. I sat down to practice my four Sunday hours, interruptible only by one drink of water and one visit to the toilet, looking forward in misery to the pupil concerts my father would find that afternoon as he did many Sunday afternoons. These were free showcases in school auditoriums of neighborhood piano teachers who had their best pupils perform, something I had begun to do, too. And my father wanted me, unremittingly, to see how it was done by others, better than I. Once I had accepted that no part of those Sundays, the day of the father, was to be designed by me, I resigned myself to the concerts as well as the long practice session.

I couldn't say I didn't like music. Unless we were fighting or sick, we all sang, even my father, who would yodel "Vesti la Giubba" with Caruso as he paced the long hall. Music appreciation was a happy hour in school where we sang together with records, "This is the symphony-y-y-y-y that Schubert wrote and never fini-i-i-ished, This is the key of C that" and we dropped it waiting to shout "Italian, Italian!," celebrating Mendelssohn. The names were dazzlingly esoteric: Mendelssohn (my father said he was Jewish, but my father said all important people were somewhere in their ancestry Jews), Saint-Saëns, Massenet, Tchaikovsky, and frowning Beethoven who wrote the thunderous "Da da da daaaaa, Da da da Daaaaa," like the voice of God.

We sang a great deal in school, which made most of us very happy, and I one of the lucky few who were aware, at that moment, of being perfectly happy. We sang "Santa Lucia," which later paced my first gondola ride and became the twin of Schubert's "Auf dem Wasser zu Singen," a curious duet that I would not for anything sever. "Funiculi, Funicula" was skating downhill fast, roaring past houses on the El, the pretty jingling and hooting of merry-go-round music. The words of some of the songs moved me inordinately and I sang them pipingly, gently, in tremolos, as their meaning dictated: "As the sun-flower turns on her god, when he sets, The same look which she turn'd when he rose" became an ideal, rarely achieved, in my life with the boys. "I sent thee late a rosy wreath, Not so much honoring thee as in the hope that by thy side it might not witheréd be. But thou thereon didst only breathe and sendst it back to me. Since when it lives and breathes, I swear it, not of itself but thee." Jonson's slightly altered song cast a long, golden light over all my life, gracing what I came to know of courtly love, of madrigals and cavalier poets, of Shakespeare's sonnets. (One of the remnants of my early musical life is the music that was played during the film of Disraeli's life, starring George Arliss; any English garden can restore it almost intact.)

In spite of some necessary and a few unnecessary bestialities, it was a fine school, P.S. 58 on Bathgate Avenue and 182nd Street, and I still miss it, which is to say I miss being the full-throated thrush, the throbbing nightingale I was there.

To return to the Sunday afternoon concerts: I knew some of the music and could sit in a mixture of contentment and embarrassment listening to the clinkers a nervous kid on the stage was striking. Some of them had demonic techniques, some of them could make really singing sounds. There were a few things I wanted to play because they were so tuneful, like the Arensky waltz and something called, with deep respect, Bach, which sounded difficult and important. When the music was boring, I could examine the girls' hair and wonder at the patience of both mother and daughter that produced cascades of curls. The white dress with lace was too much like a communion dress, the pink more appropriate. And I fervently wished I had a ring to take off my finger and put down, with a languid gesture, at the end of the keyboard before I began to play.

Much more than the concerts I hated the long walks and talk afterward. I was told, and accepted as accusations, that Marilyn, who had played that difficult Chopin étude, and Martin, who had played three Bach inventions, and Amy of that fast cross-hands piece—what's its name?—didn't go to school anymore, just stayed home and practiced six and eight hours a day, not like me who practiced only two every day, even Saturday when I had no school, and only four on Sunday. If I stopped going to school—all I had to do was announce to my teachers that I wasn't coming back—and practiced all day, he and I would, someday, travel around the world giving concerts. Striding in the evening winds, his coat open and flapping like an old-fashioned cape, he looked wild, carried away, like Mr. Rochester in *Jane Eyre*, like Heath-cliff. He talked of concerts in Paris and London where all I had to do was play the piano on a stage—the pupil concerts in which I now performed were important preparation—and he would take care of getting the halls and collecting the money. We would be rich and travel all over the world, have beautiful clothing, and be admired by important people. I saw it all at first like becoming a princess, a young Queen Victoria gesturing daintily in lacy white gloves to the multitudes. After a good number of these Sunday evening walks into a make-believe that I enjoyed less and less, I began to grow distinctly uneasy, wanting to tear away from him. The message across my head—the same ticker tape that told me that my father liked to walk alone, several paces in front of the baby carriage my mother was pushing, my brother and I at either side, in order to be seen by passersby as a young unmarried man—reappeared to insist that this, too, was wrong. Never was there any mention of a mother, a brother, a baby sister to share the wealth and fame; they were erased, they didn't exist.

For him, but not for me. Often disgruntled, often resentful, often aching to be free of them, I wouldn't have them disappear, not for being as rich and famous as Mary Pickford. Had someone suggested that I "loved" them, I would have spat. They were my landscape, my geography, and what, who, would I be without them? I listened as he elaborated on his glorious theme, repainting his warm colors as the darker reality of a life controlled into infinity by him alone: being called "Luna Park" when I smiled; told not to be crazy when I wanted to do something, anything, of which he didn't approve; practicing eight hours a day; burning bowels and diarrhea before each concert; having no street to run to or my mother to argue for me. How would I know whether my brother grew up with two stumpy front teeth, broken when he cracked down on the steering rod of his sled, belly-whopping on the icy hill of 179th Street? Would my sister ever grow out of sitting hunched in a corner, her eyes tight shut as she covered her ears while my brother and I screamed at each other? She was a smart little kid, and I wasn't going to give up my ambition to teach her to read, to make her the wonder child of the block who would dazzle the librarians when they gave her the first library-card test. I had to finish a stuffed doll I was making for her in school and finish hemstitching a camisole; I would never wear it, I didn't know what it was for, but the orderly stitches becoming a pretty row had become as satisfying as drawing. I certainly didn't want to miss the backyard of P.S. 58 when it was a summer vegetable garden where I could watch my kohlrabi and lettuce grow and carry them home in both hands stretched before me as if they were boxes of precious jewels for my mother, the queen. No, he couldn't really have me; I had another kind of life to lead, whatever it would be.

His distressing fantasy took on tangents that I felt were connected to his ambitious dream, though I couldn't clearly see or understand them. Although the games boys and girls played were usually distinctly masculine or feminine, there were some games we played together, "ring-a-levio," stoopball, hide-and-seek, races on foot or skates around the block. Seeing my grinning, sweaty face coming around the corner neck and neck with a boy one early fall evening on his return from work, my father told me to come upstairs right away. The supper lecture that night was directed at me; I was getting too old to run around like an unleashed thing with the boys, that's what street girls did. If he caught me ever again playing with the boys, I would not be permitted to go into the street after supper, not even to sit on the stoop embroidering my dish towel and singing "Cecilia" and "All Alone" with the other girls. I promised while I began quickly to figure times safe and unsafe for the forbidden games.

One of those same early evenings, a Friday, no school tomorrow, the Paradise of Saturday promising and three cents for the weekly ice-cream cone in our hands, we ran right after supper to Mrs. Katz's candy store. We were several, including tough Helen. As we approached the store we saw an unusual crowd, much larger than the usual Friday night clusters. They were gathered around a tall, elderly gentleman with smooth pale hair, as well dressed as the De Santises' gangster uncle. With wide gestures and in a German accent we recognized from vaudeville skits, he was inviting everyone in sight to take candy, order ice cream, cigarettes, anything. He was paying. And he did, putting down ten- and twenty-dollar bills that Mrs. Katz quickly hid. I watched him, I watched her, and realized that she was taking much too much money from him, claiming that a handful of Tootsie Rolls and a few fistfuls of Hershey bars had exhausted ten dollars and she needed more. He gave her more from a thick roll of bills, thicker than I had ever seen, while the kids and a few adults pushed one another and roared for chunks of halvah, five-cent ice-cream cones, packs of cigars and cigarettes, handfuls of gum. I couldn't understand what the stranger was doing or why. Was he drunk? But I had never seen a drunk other than Mary Sugar

Bum, and maybe she was only crazy, old. I was afraid of what he was doing; it was craziness, like the wild talk and rolling eyes of Mrs. Silverberg the night they took her away, and I hated what Mrs. Katz was doing to him. I started pulling away, back toward our house, calling to Helen, who had made her way into the middle of the crowd, to come back with me. On hearing her name, he paused and, peering at me, said, *"Ach, die schoene Helene. I know that face; there's music in that face,"* and continued to stare at me. Such extraordinary praise I had seen only in poems, and it didn't belong to me. I stayed, though, and watched the noisy, crowding grabbing as he stripped more bills off the plump pack, looking over at me now and then, calling, *"Die schoene Helene."* Suddenly my father, who usually kept himself aristo-cratically away from street life, appeared, dragged me off by the arm, hurried me through the street and up the stairs. I had done nothing, absolutely nothing, but stand with the other kids; I hadn't even taken a stick of gum for free. I tried to tell him so as he flung me into a kitchen chair, but he wouldn't let me. It poured out of his black mouth: I was not to go out of the house for a week, not to the street, to no friend's house, not to the Hermans or the Haskells or the Roths or the Santinis, not even to school, he shrieked, his pale face sharpened like a murderer's. No library, no movies that Saturday; no concert on Sunday.

On Monday, after my brother had gone to school, I asked my mother what I had done. She didn't think I had done anything wrong; my father was in one of his nervous fits, unusually long this time. Don't worry. I did; we were learning fractions and percentages and I was having trouble with them. By next week they would be learning something else and I would never catch up. In spite of my mother's assurances that I had done nothing, I didn't believe her. I must have done something to be punished so severely that I couldn't even go to school, but what it was I couldn't imagine. I went over every detail of that evening, over and over again, and understood little except that it was bad and I was central to the badness, having disturbed my father's dream in some way. Our suppers were altogether silent that week, no one spoke in the evenings, not even my brother, who had taken one timid piece of candy at Mrs. Katz's and was afraid that he, too, might be discovered and put under house arrest.

The return to school was not triumphant. I had been deeply shamed by being yanked around publicly, like a bad baby about to be spanked and ashamed of the terrible thing I had done, something everyone but me could see on my face. I handed our teacher the note my mother gave me to say I had been sick— another lie—and slid into my seat, my eyes down so I wouldn't see *their* eyes looking at me.

14

Tony and Company

The end of that term, the end of the sixth grade, was a decisive one. Some of us would go on to 7A and two years at P.S. 57 on 181st at Crotona Avenue, the smart ones would go to "rapid advance," a junior high school where three years were accomplished in two. I hoped and prayed to the bearded God, making him extravagant promises of eternal goodness, no more lies, no more fights, total perfection, because I was afraid arithmetic would do me in. It did. I had to submit to the spotty sympathy of friends who had made it, to the "we don't care, do we" of friends who hadn't, to the compassionate murmurs addressed to my disappointed mother. Miss Torrence was some consolation. As we walked down the street from school the day the "rapid advance" selections were made, she said that judging a person's capacity to learn from a few mistakes in arithmetic was very foolish. Why didn't they take into account the fact that I knew more books and poems than anyone else in the school and wrote the best compositions? A few teachers disagreed with the selections; they thought I should have been on the "fast" list, as she did, and were annoyed because Gracie Makerios hadn't made it either, just because she had a slight Greek accent. Why hadn't they taken into account how much she had accomplished in only four years in school?

My father's reaction was monumental, even for him. Although he was eager to pull me out of school, this was a searing wound to his vanity. He said I was inattentive in school; not true, I always got A for attention. He said I didn't try; not true, I always got A for effort. Maybe I was more stupid than he thought, maybe there was something wrong with a head that couldn't cope with simple numbers. Or maybe—he paused—I did all this to spite him, contrived to flunk whatever tests or standards so that he would be humiliated in the eyes of the neighbors, in the eyes of the men in his shop whom he had told I was going into rapid advance classes. It was an absorbing, titillating new idea, worth considering in a future context, but here so absurd that my mother called to him from the kitchen not to make such a fool of himself and we'd had enough of the whole matter. That went for my brother, too, in case he should be thinking of taunting me.

I marched with my fellow discards a new route, altogether free of my brother, who remained in P.S. 58. The walk was now past my tree on 179th Street, up Arthur Avenue, past the synagogue to 180th Street, east on 180th and the big Italian fruit and vegetable store, its bins burbling with shapes and shining colors. Near Belmont the wallpaper store with pictures, the same one over and over again of blue birds in bamboo cages, and then the red brick building with a big yard, P.S. 57, at Crotona. We picked up a few people from other sixth-grade schools along the way, not too many girls. But maybe I only noticed the boys. One of them was Marty Green, who looked like Huckleberry Finn, like the boys on the *Saturday Evening Post* covers with spiky hair, freckles, and one knicker leg falling to his ankles. A jabberer, a joker, a jumpy walker like a marionette; cute. And distinctly not my type, which was sleek and sloe-eyed like Ramon Navarro, or like thin-faced Chopin in a sad, soft cloud of hair. Worst of all, Marty had no dignity. He jumped around me, made dumb loud jokes in my direction, and, most odd, began to follow me, silently and at a discreet distance, home from school. Flattered and preening, trying to walk with my feet pointed forward, not to walk like Charlie Chaplin as my father said I did, I found the situation distinctly worrisome. Knowing something of hopeless yearnings for one word from Federico De Santis, for a glance from Helen's ravishing high-school brother, I was sorry for him. And afraid. Even if I decided to acknowledge interest in him, what would I say? What must I do as his girl friend? Would I have to wind myself around him like the couples we spied on in the park, necking and petting, playing gidgee, even? Could I kiss him as I did my little sister, or would I have to kiss him as they did in the movies, mouth to mouth and breathing hard? This being followed at a distance, which I liked, I also disliked because it was a little like being spied on by my brother, who had decided with my father that I was boy-crazy and becoming a flapper and had to be watched. Somewhere in the confusion there was a sense also of waiting for a more challenging adventure; much as I hated them, I did have breasts, inappropriate for a freckled boy of eleven or twelve. The Love of My Life had to be at least fifteen, suave and slick, surrounded by gaggles of girls over whom I would triumph brilliantly, like Gloria Swanson. (I found him, or invented him, but that's a later story.)

In the meantime more damned trouble, more and more, with being "felt up." Every once in a while my recalcitrant stormy hair had to be cut professionally and I was sent to my father's barber, Tony (they were all Tony, as all Mexican gardeners are Jesus), on Tremont Avenue and Washington, usually after a Saturday

morning visit to the library nearby, a pleasure spoiled in anticipated dread. Tony was short and smiled like a villain, calling me a
nice pretty girl he would make even prettier, as he spread a huge,
imprisoning cloth over me. He was extraordinarily dexterous,
combing and snipping with one hand while his other explored
under the sheet, slowly, carefully, with gentle pinches and soft
circles around my imprisoned breasts. When I squirmed to pull
myself away from his hand, he laughingly warned me that if I
didn't sit still he might cut my ear. So I sat still, irritated with
time that now moved so slowly when at other times it moved so
fast; trying to concentrate on his accent and in my mind mimic it;
staring at the bottles of barber tonic on the mirror ledge; staring
into the mirror to see if it would betray his creeping hand. No,
the sheet was spread too wide and taut. There was nothing to be
said; he was my elder and mustn't be rebuked. Anyhow, how did
I know that this wasn't the way all girls got haircuts? It was a
doubtful thing, but the doubtful, weird, ununderstandable, and
erratic were everywhere I looked and touched; almost every
experience carried its shadow of madness except the library and
the movies.

After the interminable infuriating session at the barber shop, I
wouldn't eat lunch. My mother wasn't, of course, to be told what
had happened, but I was furious with her for sending me to Tony,
and it would worry her if I didn't eat, an extraordinary occur-
rence, especially when she had cooked a pot of barley soup with
lima beans and dried mushrooms, one of my favorites. She said I
couldn't go to the movies if I didn't eat, upon which my brother
threw down his spoon and began to yell at both of us because he
couldn't go to the movies without me. My mother relented about
the movies but said we couldn't have a nickel for candy, half for
him, half for me. So he kicked and kept kicking me during the
news, which didn't interest him at all, and managed to be espe-

cially offensive during the day's love scenes when he hissed into my ear, "Mush! Mush! Icky mush!" while I was melting into the screen.

It was a surprise but no longer a shock to find other men, men I knew as fathers, capable of acting like Tony. Mr. Silverberg, whose wife was still institutionalized, often came to visit his cousins next door, the Goodmans, and visited us as well. One early Friday evening, he asked my mother if he could take me to the movies, the expensive movie that also had vaudeville. To forestall a refusal, I quickly babbled out that I had practiced my whole two hours and I didn't have to get up early to go to school the next day and I had lots of time for homework. Please. Please. She said I could go; wash my face, comb my hair, change my dress. I hurried, afraid my father would come home to stop me and Mr. Silverberg. We were lucky and got to Loew's without meeting him. Mr. Silverberg was one of those men who looked like an old baby, with the infantile features and worried looks of a Child Jesus who knew there was trouble in store for him; he was round and soft, like a grandmother, but I liked his brown suit and the tan tie attached to his very white Arrow collar. It seemed as if he had dressed up for me and I was glad I had on my concert dress. At the box office the immense dignity of having a special ticket bought for me, rather than the childish Saturday scramble of proffered dimes and the "Take us in, mister, please" to one of the few adults who dared the matinee mob of kids. Mr. Silverberg bought me a Hershey bar, a whole Hershey bar for myself, and asked me where I'd like to sit. I suggested the orchestra, timidly, since I had rarely been anywhere but the balcony, where kids were required to sit in the Belmont Theater. He helped me off with my coat, asked me if I was comfortable and could I see all right. I muttered something out of my overwhelmed face and then the vaudeville show came on, unfortunate because I hadn't had time to prepare for one of the *mudne* moods that vaudeville plunged me into. I adored, was ready to give my life to, the clowns and the jugglers and the young people who sang and danced snappily in curly costumes and glistening slippers. When the old men in baggy pants came on to make lame jokes that no one laughed at and the too-jolly women in pink tight dresses, like swollen frankfurters, sang in harsh, flat sounds, I would—were I with my mother—hide my face not to be part of their shame. But I was not with my mother, who had, in any case, vowed never to go to the movies with me after I hid from half the vaudeville acts and cried all through *The Gold Rush*. With my grown-up escort I sat and smiled straight ahead of me, applauding as he did, laughing when I thought I should, being as little odd as possible, although it still hurt to hear the dead jokes, the hectic rough singing, and feel all the frantic trying.

The movie was with Nita Naldi, my favorite vamp, black hair, black eyes, black veils, black beads, a glorious creature who moved like a big snake, who didn't talk much but just looked out of her long, smoky eyes and withered all but the strongest heroes, who managed through riveting hours to resist her sorcery and survive to marry the blond heroine. Sitting with Nita Naldi, my chest heavy with her beads and magical amulets, on a broad throne, one hand covered with rings dropping languidly over a chair arm carved like a lion's head, I felt a touch on my thigh, the hand of Mr. Silverberg. I hoped it was some sort of accident and waited. The hand crept up, tried to get into my bloomers, but the elastic was too tight. It tried to get into my bloomers from above but my dress belt, pulled to make my waist small, got in his way, too. He unbuttoned the back of my dress, put his arm and hand in, and began to finger the one breast he could reach, flattened under the ribbon, which he tried to peel away; it was held firmly by two big diaper pins. He went back to my bloomers, stroking on the cloth. I crossed my legs tightly, which gave him one buttock to work on. His other hand seemed to be busy in his pants. I couldn't turn to see but I could sense the familiar trembling.

When the movie was over, he helped me on with my coat and in the course of the walk home made grown-up conversation: Wasn't that a good movie? He always enjoyed Nita Naldi, didn't I? Wasn't that clown with the electric-bulb nose funny? I answered in monosyllables, wondering once more at the perfidy of adults who could do such dirty things in the dark and then talk as if nothing had happened. He didn't ask me not to tell my parents, he knew I wouldn't. When we reached 2029, I asked him to go up without me, please to tell my parents I would be right up. The stairs were dark and I wanted no more groping, no more trying to squeeze myself into a tight ball, no more of his bland voice or his sharp-edged collar; no more. I stood for a minute or two in front of the street lamp. It had begun to snow and watching the snow flakes dance on their golden stage of light helped erase Mr. Silverberg. When I got upstairs I could say to my parents, yes, it was a good show and a good picture; yes, I had enjoyed myself, very much; yes, I had thanked him; yes, Mr. Silverberg was very nice to take me.

The sequence is unclear but within a few months Frankie Polanski, then about seventeen, was arrested and jailed and his sister Carola, a year younger, disappeared for a couple of days, reappeared, and left again. The Polanskis, our janitors, lived in a basement flat near the coal cellar and the mammoth stoves that made the hot water and steam heat, their one visible window below the level of the street at the side of the stoop. They had a bad-tempered curly white dog and three children, Frankie, Carola, and Stella, the youngest, who was somewhat ahead of me in school and a good girl who did her homework and ran errands for her mother. Neither Mr. Polanski, almost invisible in his cellar life, nor Mrs. Polanski spoke English except for a few barely recognizable warnings and curses when she found chalk marks on the stoop or a broken ball discarded in the hallway. She was tiny and had thin light-brown Polish hair, like my mother, like the gaggles of cleaning women who now board the city's buses, chattering in Polish, at eleven o'clock at night. She walked quickly, bent forward, propelled by a ferocity of purpose. When she scrubbed the stairs, all five flights, on her knees and skated on rags in her bare feet to polish the landings, we didn't dare pass her, didn't dare make a mark on her pristine stairs, no matter what the urgency, hunger or toilet. That went for adults, too, who humbly apologized as the discontented wrinkles twisted into "Sonnamabeech! *Pshakref!*"

Since my mother was her only Polish tenant, we had fair doses of Mrs. Polanski when her children were in trouble. Both Frankie and Carola were practiced truants, and when the truant officer came around, ununderstandable, terrifying, Mrs. Polanski rang our bell as if it were a fire alarm and then ran into the courtyard to shout my mother down. We were never permitted to go with her, it was none of our business; anyhow, we knew they were truants and what happened to truants. Hanging around the basement window, we often heard beating and shouting, Stella rushing up her stairs to cry on the stoop. No effect on Frankie and Carola; they continued to pursue their secret, free-roaming lives.

We hadn't seen Frankie at all for some time when the boys' admiring grapevine reported that he had been arrested along with a couple of his gang for stealing—what, where, we didn't know—and was in prison. Those days Mrs. Polanski sat in our kitchen—only after the stairs had been cleaned and the landings shined—crying and questioning, all in Polish. Nor was the report to our father when he came home helpful, also recounted in Polish. We gathered slowly, bit by bit, that my mother had told Mrs. P. to go downtown on the El to where many Polish people lived, on First and Second avenues, around 7th and 8th streets, and to ask them to take her to the Polish immigrant center. There she would find advice and maybe a lawyer. Mrs. Polanski had never, once she came to Lafontaine, been more than two blocks from her house and was sure she would get lost on the El and the downtown streets. She didn't go and Mr. Polanski was reported to have said when his wife suggested he make the trip, "Let him rot in prison." My mother continued to be concerned about Frankie but my father was soon bored with them and announced, "Enough, enough already, about those ignorant barbarians and the criminals they breed."

Carola's sporadic returns to the street were movie scenes from pictures about bad girls in France. They always took place in the afternoon when many of us were out to watch the poised, graceful progress of the tall girl with slender hips and full breasts. No practical Buster Brown haircut for Carol, as she now called herself. Her light hair was waved in deep curves, spitcurls pasted on her forehead and around her face, almost into her long green eyes and pointing up her high cheekbones. She always had something remarkable to show: a new red patent-leather pocketbook, shining high-heeled shoes, and real money, dollars. When we asked where she had gotten the splendors, she gestured languidly. "Oh, I have a lot of friends, rich friends, who give me presents." We had no idea how such friends could be acquired, but I got some inkling from my father and his indignation when he caught a glimpse of her one Sunday afternoon, strolling vampishly, eyeing the bench sitters in the park. He didn't bother with the tact of Polish, his Yiddish fury obviously was meant for me to understand, to take warning. See, he was right. Carola had started as a "street girl," a girl who didn't go to school, who could hardly read and write, who stayed out late and hung around with boys, and now, as he knew she would, had turned into a full-fledged *nafka*. At sixteen, with beauty-parlor hair, silk stockings, and her cheap, vulgar pocketbook (his expertise extended to bags as well as shoes), what was she looking forward to? A good job? A decent husband and children? No, of course not. But in a few years she wouldn't be pretty, she would have to go into a house of *nafkas* and serve men who would beat her. And then would come the diseases and the hospitals like Bellevue where the crazy people were kept also, and finally out in the street, wrinkled and ugly, to beg at thirty.

He may have gone on, but I had stopped listening. All that stuff about disease didn't matter; he was always talking about disease, in frankfurters, in ices, in a life without prunes. Although I was vague about some of the essential details in spite of my education by Rosa and Debby, Carol's seemed an alluring life, free and rich. I decided to start practicing to be a street girl, as usual not ready but eager for the difficulties that might entail. As my first practice piece I chose Miltie of the third floor, a good runner but otherwise something of a sissy who always listened to his mother, who had forbidden him to play marbles because it made his knickers dirty, to steal or roast mickies because it was dishonest and dangerous, or ever to remove his glasses (thus he could never fight). He was measured and joyless. I picked him also because he was always standing in my way; he must like me. When the weather grew cold and there was no more singing on the stoop, we crowded into the inner letterbox hall for talk and horseplay. Watching him staring at me through his watery glasses, I said suddenly, "You wanna wrestle?" He continued to stare, not a word. "You wanna wrestle? Take off your glasses," tough, like boys beginning a fight. As if he were a puppet I was pulling, he rose from the steps, one leg up, then the other, and slowly approached me. Our audience of four or five boys, my brother among them, moved the rubber mat into the precise middle of the floor and gathered at one side of the small hall. Still a toughie, I put my hands forward, ready for grabbing, got his shoulder, and twisted him around. He lost his balance, fell, shot up in a fury of humiliation, whipped his glasses off to hand to the nearest boy, put a foot between mine, and tripped me. I fell on the stairs, sat up, put my arms around his knees, pulled, and felled him again. I jumped on top of him and we pushed, grabbed, rolled, pulled each other's hair, elbowed each other's bellies, I in my sweaty efforts noting just what it was I was pounding and how it felt. Our audience, who might ordinarily be yelling instruction and criticisms, was silent; it was an awesome event, this match with a girl, and beyond comment. When someone yelled "Chickie!" because Mr. Haskell was mounting the stoop, we leaped up, brushed our disheveled clothing, wiped our wet faces, and tried to look conversational. Fortunately Mr. Haskell was child-proof, never saw, never gave a damn, indifferent to our disordered clothing and our boiling faces. As we walked up the inner stairs to our apartment I told my brother that if he mentioned the wrestling I would tell that he had called Manny a fuck. OK. He didn't and I didn't.

The wrestling went on through a number of sessions, Miltie no longer reluctant, no longer waiting to be challenged. We made appointments. "Tomorrow, five o'clock." "No, I can't. I got Hebrew school tomorrow." "OK, Wednesday." We met and wrestled vigorously, Miltie improving mightily as we punched, shoved, and explored each other's anatomy. Until someone forgot to yell "Chickie!" before Mr. Kaplan, our morals committee, walked in on us to stare, without comment, at the octopus of flailing boy and girl limbs. He gave me a look of burning contempt, not Miltie, stepped by us and into the house to report immediately, we all knew, to my father.

As we had learned to say, we girls of almost thirteen, old enough for monthlies and "bassiers," "Then the shit hit the electric fan." My father bellowed, he stamped like the bull in *Blood and Sand*, he shook with outrage and ordered me into the bathroom for a beating. My mother yelled "No!" Folk wisdom forbade the beating of a nubile girl on her bare buttocks; it suspected a scent of pleasure. He slapped me instead, thrusting me like a top from one wall of the narrow hallway to the other with each ringing blow. When my sister ran out of the kitchen crying and tried to get between us, he stopped. My mother held on to her disapproving assistant-principal face as I went by her to my bedroom and didn't say a word when my father accused her of encouraging me to become another Carola Polanski.

The wrestling stopped and Miltie stayed away from that part of the street on which I talked or played, no longer hung around me in the school yard. It didn't matter much, I still had my other puppet, Marty, and had begun to fix my eyes and imagination on Sal Venturi, the Man of P.S. 57. He roused storms of feeling in me, a full sun of elation when I saw him alone, a sack of despair when he talked to other girls. I whirled in dreams of living with him in enchanted castles, a life of pure white satin, or, scorned, trailing after him for the rest of my dragging, boneless life. Sal had blond hair and blue eyes, an exquisite phenomenon in an Italian; he was tall, the champion of the swimming team, of the basketball team, a man of legend. He was masterful with the teachers, looking at them with a twisted smile and insolent eyes when they rebuked him for not having done his homework. The younger teachers spoke to him with the same smile and bold eyes, as if they were sharing a secret. His name was dragged into countless girl conversations, the subject of luxuriant gossip. He had, they said, several girl friends, big girls who used lipstick, with whom he played gidgee, the real thing, the big act beyond petting and muzzling.

He never did his homework, they said; he flunked tests and skipped school and didn't care because he knew how to twist the teachers around his little finger. He paid no attention to the girls in P.S. 57; his was stronger game. When I tried to speak to him, after much deliberation and gathering together my fraying courage, something inane came out, like "You think you're great, don't you? Well, I don't." He didn't seem to hear and I could have torn my tongue out. Since there was to be no conversation, I began to follow him to find out where he lived, to have a picture of his street and house, to give him a landscape. I was sly, wary, staying well behind at first until I realized that he and his gang, shoving each other into the gutter, pummmeling each other's arms, wouldn't know who I was even if it occurred to them to look back.

He lived near the Italian market a few blocks north of school in a house with a glassed-in porch (must be rich), and here I stationed myself frequent evenings, sometimes across the street, sometimes behind a nearby tree, to catch a glimpse of him and his sophisticated girl friends, to see what they did. I got to know his fat father and an uncle or a friend who played dominoes for hours on end. I learned that his mother used a wooden egg for darning socks and wished my mother had one. His plump blond sister buffed her nails as she talked with her mother. It was like looking at paintings, out of the dark street into the bright, framed light of the porch. It became evident that the porch was Sal's on weekends only so I limited my spying to Friday and Saturday nights. The high-heeled girls, undoubtedly wearing brassieres under their tight-waisted flouncy dresses, bounced around on the couches, allowing a boy's arm to rest on their shoulders for a moment before quickly shrugging it away. Mostly they laughed and ate crackers and candy and danced the Charleston. I suspected the other things would happen later with the lights turned off but I couldn't stay. It was painful, the bright liveliness; it made me an outcast, cut off from all pleasures forever and ever. I spent the rest of those evenings, and others, and much of those days, in dark caves of self-pity and gnawing jealousy.

The evenings of spying on my love resulted in heavy muttering at home. My excuse for coming in late was that I had taken a long walk and hadn't noticed the time. It was an unfortunate excuse, the long walk. Why didn't we take them together, as we used to, suggested my father. Since I had presented myself rather suddenly as an enthusiast of long walks, there was nothing I could do but let him play impresario again. Again, I was to tell my teachers that I had to quit school (they would tell the principal, nothing to it) so I could practice the piano all day. I was the best piano player on the block, he said, and the best of Mr. Stone's pupils; a respected teacher wouldn't trust just anyone to play Chopin's "Fantasie Impromptu" at his student recital, would he? And listen to this, listen. He would get rid of the old secondhand piano that the blind piano tuner said couldn't be fixed anymore without spending a lot of money and put that money down on a new piano, a real Hardman-Peck, almost as good as a Steinway. How would I like that? I said that would be very nice, telling myself it wouldn't happen. Promises held OK among kids but not among adults. They were temporary bribes, a mechanism for "get off my back" or "do what I say." What if he should actually buy a new piano, though? I would be in serious trouble: leave the school, the street, my friends, my tree, my mother, my brother, sister, the library, the movies, Crotona Park, and be his exclusively the rest of my life. The new piano became a larger and larger presence during these forced marches. He described a piano he had looked at, its size and high, new shine, the carved music rack and the big golden letters on the lid. Sounds like clear bells and no stuck notes, no buzzing lower notes. Of course, later on when I had become a concert artist we would have a huge Steinway whose top could be lifted to become a great wing. And with it would come a plush-cushioned seat that a pianist could adjust for reaching the notes and the pedals perfectly.

The piano actually, shockingly, came, wrapped in felt cloths and ropes and lifted carefully by four men with swollen muscles up the five flights of stairs, every door open to watch its progress. The dollar my mother paid the moving men, the noble size of the piano, and its luster, which emblazoned the room, were things to boast of, to show off to special friends. The glowing pedals could be touched subtly, to make soft rainbows of sound. The keys were shining white and obeyed every touch of my fingers; they made me feel like a pianist, not just a kid practicing. This piano was for Beethoven sonatas, not the "Rustle of Spring," and still the Great Threat, the Terrible Enemy. When my father came home that night, he examined the piano minutely, asking that I admire it with him, mentioning several times the unbelievable price—hundreds of dollars—and asking if I wasn't pleased and grateful. I admired, wondered at the price, and said I was very pleased to have it. Now was the time to settle down to real practicing, he said, to prepare for my career. And no more reading in bed half the night and fooling around with my stupid friends; practice would need my full strength and concentration.

The prison gates were yawning open. Each evening I was asked whether I had told my teachers I was quitting. Each evening I lied: my teacher was sick and we had a substitute who didn't know anything; the principal was off at a school conference; Miss Bender had told me my father would have to come to school himself, lose a day's work. He scorned my stories and information. I was a coward, a big mouth at home and incapable of making a simple request in school. I lied about practicing; yes I was now practicing two and a half hours a day rather than the usual two; neither my brother nor my mother informed against me; like myself, they sensed threatening developments and chose to remain silent observers. They knew my father would keep urging that I leave school. They knew I wouldn't. They watched and waited.

I was running out of lies and my father out of patience when we received a letter from Yankel. He was living in Toledo, working as a bookkeeper, and was coming to New York to see a girl he had met earlier in an English class; her father owned a big store on Grand Street. Could he stay with his dear family a couple of nights? It wasn't the skinny, pimpled boy who walked through the door. This one wore a stickpin in his tie and a ruby pinkie ring. His suit hung neatly on his full shoulders and he had stopped biting his nails. He walked through the hall, past the kitchen, and sat himself confidently at the dining room table, placing a box of chocolates in its center. No one opened the box. My mother was reluctant to accept a gift from Yankel; it was not my father's business to open boxes of candy; we didn't dare. It sat there growing taller and wider under our anxious eyes, and we finally left it as unattainable as he went on and on describing his New York girl's father's store, big, with two salesmen who measured out hundreds of yards of velvets, satins from Italy, and lace imported from France, no kitchen curtain stuff, mind you, and in a busy, choice location. How was business in Toledo, my father asked. Was Yankel going to get his citizenship papers soon? Did he think he could get his mother over this year; my father's landsmen would of course help out. It grew late, the conversation dwindled. The tea glasses were washed and put back into the kitchen cabinet, the lights went out, and then the long night silence, dotted by my parents' snorts and whistles.

The folding cot had been taken out of the closet and arranged for Yankel under the rubber plant that, by now, almost touched the ceiling. As usual, my brother was asleep as soon as his head fell to the pillow, my sister was already long asleep. I took my shoes off but not my dress. Yankel had made a fuss about how big and pretty I'd become, almost a woman, and I'd better watch out for the boys. I knew that kind of praise from the watchman of the factory next door, from a Bianchi relative who owned a bakery on Catherine Street and courted us girls with Italian almond cookies, and I knew Yankel. And I waited. My brother, a talkative dreamer, muttered a conflict about "immies," the choicest of marbles; my sister smacked her lips as if she were sucking a lollipop. From the farthest room came the muffled duet of my mother's high rattle and my father's deeper, calmer snores. The wind shook the window shade now and then. Nothing else. I was beginning to fall asleep, still fully dressed, when I heard a light sound at the door, the loose doorknob stuttering as it turned, the door creaking open slowly. There was Yankel, his short American underwear clear and white in the dark. Before he could approach the bed I jumped up and ran at him, hissing, "Get out! Get the hell out of here!" One startled look and he disappeared. I pushed the chair against the door just to make sure, although I doubted he would try again, got undressed and under the covers, but I didn't sleep, hot with hatred of Yankel and my father. My father, like myself, slept lightly; he must have known what Yankel was doing and had done before, and Bessie, too. He permitted it because they were Family on whom he had spent considerable effort and money, eager to get them to New York: Yankel, Bessie, and later numerous sisters in black and brown sateen stretched over broad horizons of bosom, and the unforgettable Sarita. (The stringent tightening of immigration laws kept Sarita, the last, for a longish period in Cuba before her importation to New York. She was a bandy-legged, pitted thing, adroit and assiduous in her flattery of Uncle and his son, who suddenly found himself with a generous allowance to take Sarita, a good number of years older than himself, to the movies and ice-cream parlors. My brother

hated "old" Sarita, whose presence was interfering with his growing reputation as the Don Juan of the block. To escape her, and to
parallel my later freedom, he signed on as cabin boy with a
Caribbean freighter. She hung on, encouraged by Uncle, who was
hinting at an ultimate marriage as soon as my brother could earn
a good living—he was fifteen at the time. My mother loathed her
as ugly and a hypocrite and my few encounters with her revealed
a stupid, transparent conniver. We were all saved from her when
she had an agonizing attack of abdominal pain. One of my
friends, an intern at Beth Israel, drove us there in his father's car.
It didn't take long to determine that she was suffering a flare-up
of a well-ensconced case of gonorrhea. She couldn't stay there;
Bellevue was the hospital for venereal diseases. Get her out of here
and up there. Now. Quick. Shocked but undiscouraged, my
father found her a room and a job after months of treatment, and
since his son would absolutely, definitely, not have anything to
do with her, searched out a lonely, elderly *shlemiel* for her to
marry.)

There are several variations of a story in which a dying Jew is
making out his will with the help of a friend. "But," the friend
protests, "if you leave the store to your brother Ben, your money
in the bank to your brother Sol, and your house to your sister
Rosie, what's left for your wife and children, your family?"
"What family? What are you talking about? Rosie, Sol, Ben,
that's my family."

This was my father and his Family, who obviously had the
additional privilege of using me. It was he who was making me a
"street girl" for anyone in the Family, a thing that had no
feelings, no thoughts, no choices. There I was to lie, a slice of fresh
cornbread, a chicken leg, a snack before sleep. Triumphant over
Yankel and furious with them all—why didn't my sharp mother
suspect something and protect me?—I began to put my hands on

my hips when I answered back, like Carol Polanski. Asked where
I was going, I began with "Out," and built up to "None of your
business." I refused to take walks with *him*, vengeful and dead
scared with the new piano shining at me, of his wild imaginings.
When I caught him following me to the Italian market section to
be nearer Sal, I changed direction to a distant library that was
open in the evening. Though I could not take books out, I was
allowed to sit and read, catching glimpses of him pacing back and
forth at the entrance in the brisk night. He managed to stay a
block or two behind me as we walked, but he knew that I knew
he was there. When my mother protested that our walks were
growing too long and late, he said I was getting fat and lazy and
didn't so much need sleep as exercise. The practicing diminished,
my mother a weekday witness to the fact. All she said was "What
a shame. So much that piano cost. What a shame." Much of the
nonpracticing time was spent across from the corner candy store
that was Sal's hangout, adoring the way a lit cigarette dangled
from his lower lip, adoring and hating the way he stepped in
front of a neighborhood girl, standing straight and close, staring
down at her until she moved away with a small smile on her face.

Imagining, planning, rehearsing, practicing stances of courage,
I announced one Sunday morning, not directly to my father but
rather into the air around him, that I was not going to the
student concert that afternoon, nor was I, anymore, going to
practice four hours on Sunday morning, with time out for one
toilet trip and one drink of water. Riding on the wind I had
churned up in myself, I continued: Two hours was enough for
any day; I wasn't going to be a concert pianist and maybe not
even play in Mr. Stone's next concert. My brother and sister
slipped out the door and down the stairs; my mother began to
rattle pots and dishes in the kitchen. The big battle between us
was joined, very much as I had imagined it would be. It was he
who decided such important matters, not I. What did a thirteen-

year-old flapper (he liked to be up to date in his English), a girl
who had a head only for boys, know about great rich careers open
to talents like mine? Carnegie Hall was full of people every night
paying to listen to children younger than myself who made
hundreds of dollars for each performance. I answered that I didn't
have that much talent, I knew it and so should he. Came the
expected roar: What did I know about talent and how it could be
developed with enough practice? I was not, not, not going to
leave school to practice and he could do what he liked about it.
Anyhow, he had lied to me; I had found out that it wasn't easy to
remove a pupil from school without getting into trouble with
truant officers. I had a right to stay in school and I was going to
stay, maybe even finish high school. High school? Sure, one year
of commercial high school to learn typing and stenography, and
then, if that was the kind of life I wanted, find a job to support
myself and pay back the cost of the new piano, the big tombstone
that would stand there to remind me of the hundreds of dollars,
saved carefully over the years, the family deprived of many
things, only to be wasted by me. Dumped like potato peelings
into a garbage can, spilled like muddy rain into a sewer. I didn't
answer and walked out.

The ticker tape in my head busily clicking observations about
power and vanity, theirs and mine, and yet knowing nothing, I
went on the day of my graduation from elementary school to
change my child's library card for one that permitted me to use
the downstairs room for adults. Some writer there would tell me
what Louisa May Alcott couldn't, nor Dickens nor the children's
biographies of Mozart and Beethoven. Where the titles came
from I don't know but I had ready a mental list of books to take
from the adult shelves and found them: Knut Hamsun's *Hunger*,
Hugo's *Les Misérables*, Nietzsche's *Thus Spake Zarathustra*, the
plays of Chekhov. Armed with these mighty weapons, I would
know, I would understand. The clotted brambles would melt

away from the secret door and I would be in the adult garden of clean colors and shapes where everything had its own unchanging name; white-petaled truth always truth, the slender trees with silvery bark always promises kept, the mazes of love and sex clearly marked, brilliantly illustrated and immutable. Anyhow, it was a proud thing to be turning the pages of such great thoughts and emotions, and although they didn't teach me enough—just what was it Zarathustra was preaching? why were all those people mooning and yearning for Moscow?—they were pushing me, little by little, I hoped, toward that garden of crystal clarity. The books grew heavier, some not helpful at all— Dostoevski's brothers Karamazov were as irrational as the people around me—some, like Chekhov's stories, confirming in whispers things I almost half knew about people.

As I was reading Chekhov's "The Darling" one morning, envying her fullness of devotion, contemptuous of her dopiness, I felt as if I were losing urine, without the usual warning sensations except a heaviness in my lower belly. When I took off my bloomers in the bathroom, I saw a few red drops of blood on them and on my thigh. I called to my mother, astonished and frightened; maybe this, not going blind or crazy, was the result of masturbating. She said, smiling, that it was my monthlies and slapped me hard on the face. She had not been particularly friendly since my practicing on the new piano had diminished, but she hadn't seethed or boiled like my father. So why hit me now, what had I done? Was this some sort of punishment? For not practicing enough? For reading instead of going to the grocery store? For not watching my little sister carefully enough? For running after Sal? Why? I was back, slapped back from the growing confidence of being over thirteen to the bewilderments of eight and nine. It was months later, after I had learned to use and wash, reuse and rewash the strips of torn sheet she gave me, that she explained the slap; it was to restore a girl's circulation and

all mothers did it in the Old Country. I was relieved but un-
forgiving; she could have told me sooner, and what was this Old
Country junk in a woman who scorned so many of its practices?

It was a day in May. I had achieved my first menstrual period,
my white wedding dress tree on 179th Street had covered its sky
with blossoms. In the library that Saturday morning were my
two favorite librarians, the young woman with long blond hair
twisted in a satiny band around her head who spoke English as
Miss Bender did, as I was determined to, even though my friends
called me a "show-off" and "teacher's pet"; the word "affected"
was not in their vocabulary. The other favoirte librarian was a
short woman who always wore a brown dress with a lace collar
and brown shoes. She had puffs of brown hair and round brown
eyes and I thought of her as one of the plump brown birds I saw
in Crotona Park. She spoke with a slight accent, nothing like the
cadences I heard on Lafontaine, not marked enough to mimic.
She was intensely interested in what I was selecting, what I had
chosen to take home. *War and Peace*? She looked doubtful, but
said to try it anyway. *The Great God Brown*, maybe not, but it,
too, was worth trying. She never said absolutely no; a good
pedagogue, she let me glean what I could out of any choice I
made. She must have sensed, as well, how proud I was to be
carrying these ponderous works by masters through the street,
not on skates anymore, but on foot, like the college student I
meant to be mistaken for.

Just before lunch and the movies, my mother asked me to try
on the dress she had been making for me, a surprise. It *was* a
surprise, no loose, shapeless pongee dress with a sailor collar, the
usual summer dress-up dress. This was of thin voile printed in
irregular boxes of blue and lemon yellow, no collar, peter pan or
sailor, just narrow ties at the open neck. It was shaped, pinched in
under my breasts, narrowing down to a waist, billowing out in a

gathered skirt, covering my knees. It was a woman's dress. I wore it when we went walking in the park the next afternoon, refusing to put on a sweater. I heard little and saw less; aware only of the tucks on my ribs, the sloping seams at the sides, the swing of the skirt as it brushed my knees. I held my naked, collarless neck stiff and high, placed my feet straight before me, step after step, careful to avoid the Charlie Chaplin turned-out foot-slap my father derided. My waist was a golden ring, my sides as I stroked them had the curved perfection of antelope's horns. My arms below the puffed sleeves were cream-colored velvet. I approved of the taste of all the strokers and pinchers. I understood what they felt, felt it myself as I continued to stroke my superb sides. I saw Sal Venturi at the stoop of 2029, waiting adoringly, humbly, his eyes rolled up like a saint waiting to be pulled up to Heaven. After a slow while I would emerge, gazing at him quizzically, mockingly, one eyebrow raised above a crooked little smile. Or—there was a boundless world of choices opening around me—take his arm and walk with him into a pink twilight. The next time Mr. Silverberg offered to take me to the movies I would suggest that we go to the Chinks first, like a real date, and push his hand away firmly when it began to crawl. Or let it crawl while I laughed at him. I might let Tony play his finger games under the sheet or punch his round belly. I might say "Son of a bitch" or even "You fucking bastard" to the humpbacked watchman if he tried to pinch my ass as I passed the factory, or dance around him, my skirt swirling flirtatiously, as he lumbered toward me. The next time I went to Helen Roth's house, her high-school brother would kneel and lay at my feet a sheaf of long-stemmed red roses. Federico De Santis and his brother Berto would stick daggers into each other for rivalrous love of me.

I was ready for all of them and for Rudolph Valentino; to play, to tease, to amorously accept, to confidently reject. Lolita, my twin, was born decades later, yet a twin of the thirteen-and-a-

half-year-old striding through Crotona Park, passing the spiky
red flowers toward a kingdom of mesmerized men—young, old,
skinny, fat, good-looking, ugly, well dressed, shabby, bachelors,
fathers—all her subjects. As desirable as Gloria Swanson, as steely
as Nita Naldi, as winsome as Marion Davies, she was, like them,
invincible and immortal.